PIANO · VOCAL · GUITAR

Irish Songs

ISBN-13: 978-1-4234-1138-3
ISBN-10: 1-4234-1138-2

HAL•LEONARD®
CORPORATION

7777 W. BLUEMOUND RD. P.O. BOX 13819 MILWAUKEE, WI 53213

Visit Hal Leonard Online at
www.halleonard.com

AT THE BALL OF KIRRIEMUIR

Words and Music by FRED ARTHUR
and AL STANLEY

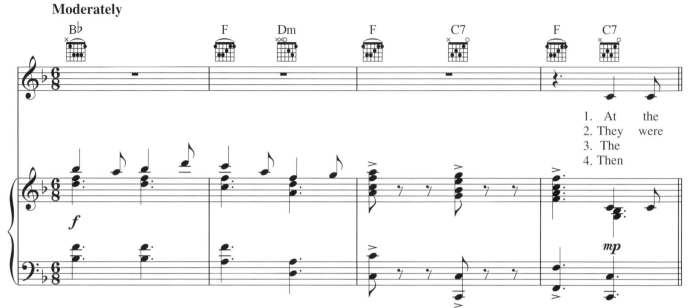

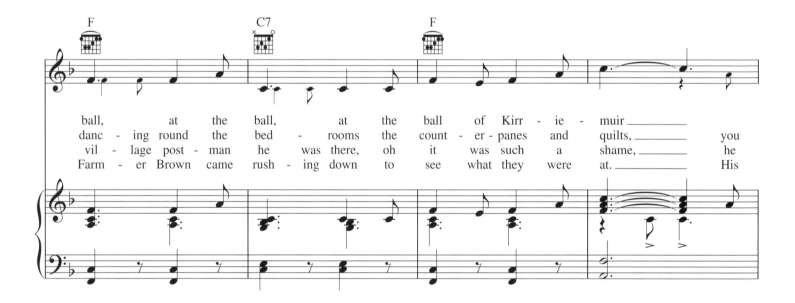

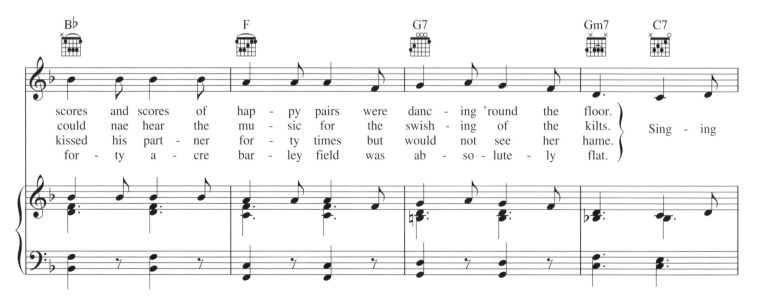

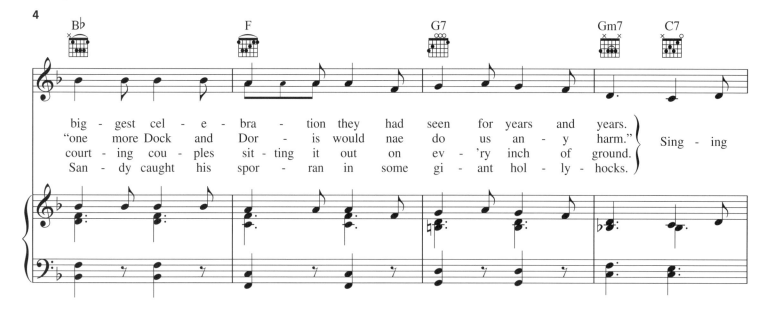

biggest cel-e-bra-tion they had seen for years and years.
"one more Dock and Dor-is would nae do us an-y harm."
court-ing cou-ples sit-ting it out on ev-'ry inch of ground.
San-dy caught his spor-ran in some gi-ant hol-ly-hocks.

Sing-ing

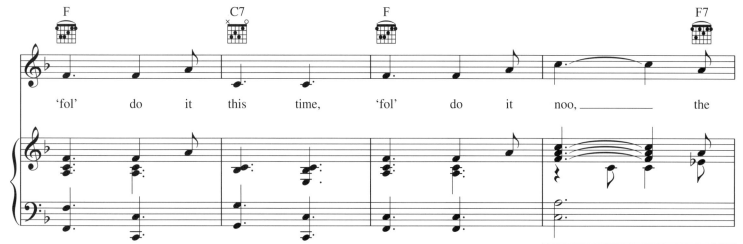

'fol' do it this time, 'fol' do it noo, _____ the

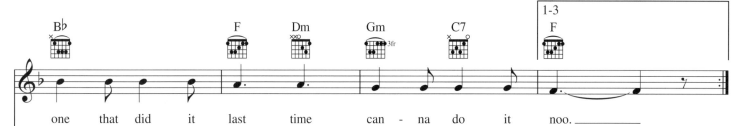

one that did it last time can-na do it noo. _____

noo. _____ 5. It looked so fun-ny hang-ing there that ev-'ry-bod-y

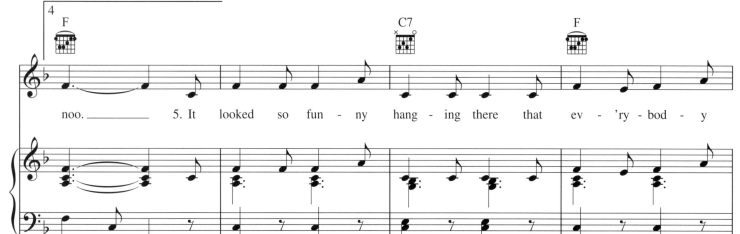

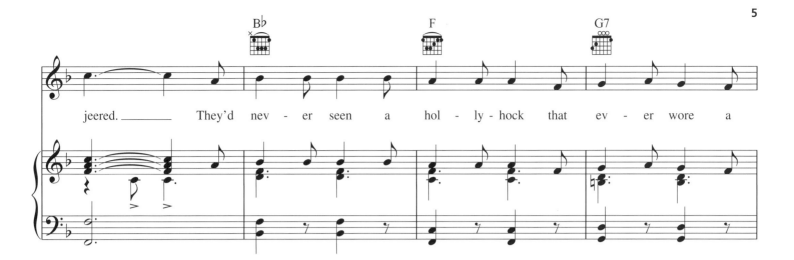

jeered. _____ They'd nev - er seen a hol - ly - hock that ev - er wore a

beard. Sing - ing 'fol' do it this time, 'fol' do it noo, _____ the

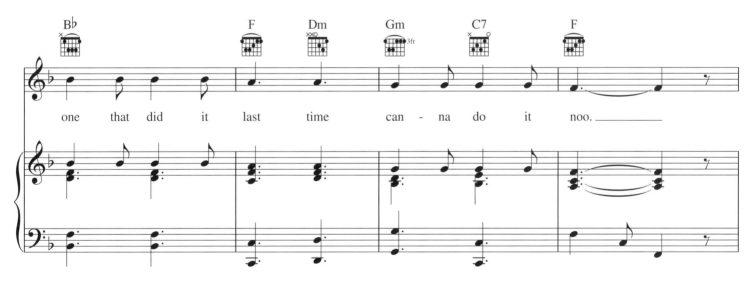

one that did it last time can - na do it noo. _____

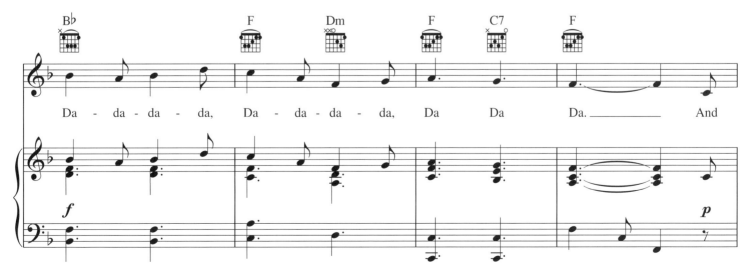

Da - da - da - da, Da - da - da - da, Da Da Da. _____ And

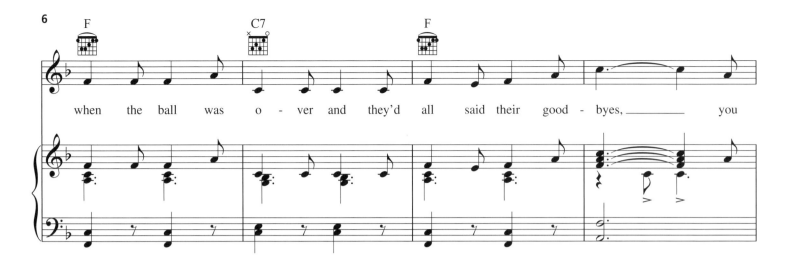

when the ball was o - ver and they'd all said their good - byes, _____ you

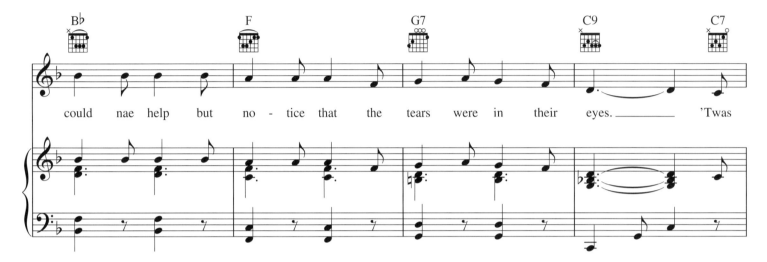

could nae help but no - tice that the tears were in their eyes. _____ 'Twas

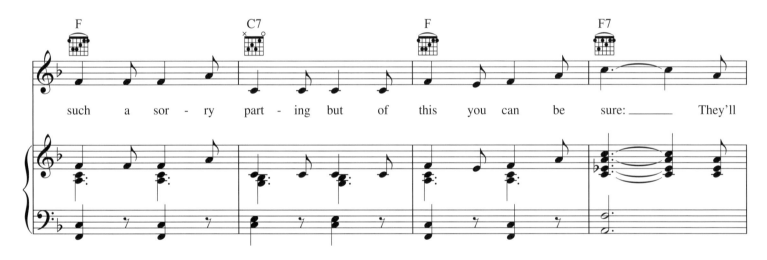

such a sor - ry part - ing but of this you can be sure: _____ They'll

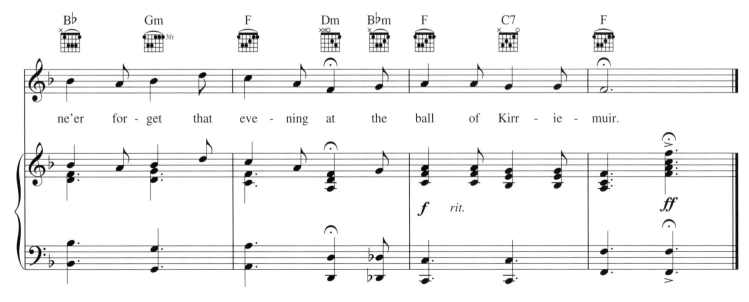

ne'er for - get that eve - ning at the ball of Kirr - ie - muir.

AT THE END OF THE RAINBOW

Words and Music by FAY SARGENT
and NOEL PIERCE

life is sad and drea-ry and hearts are sad and wea-ry,

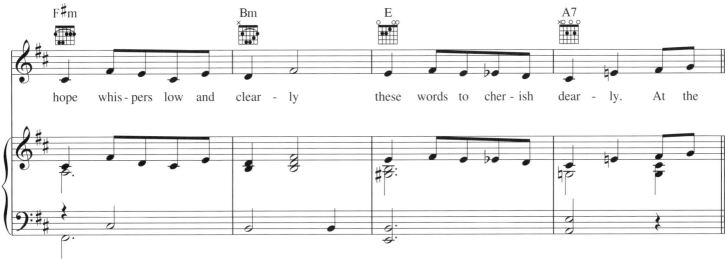

hope whis-pers low and clear-ly these words to cher-ish dear-ly. At the

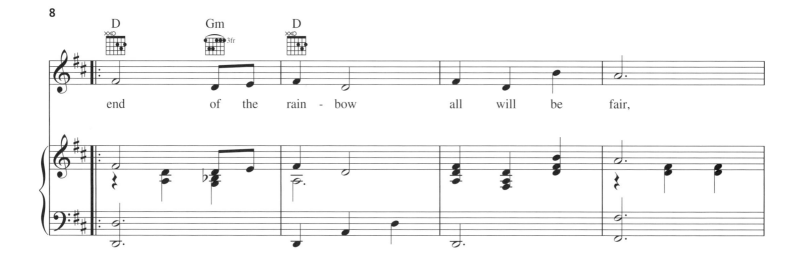

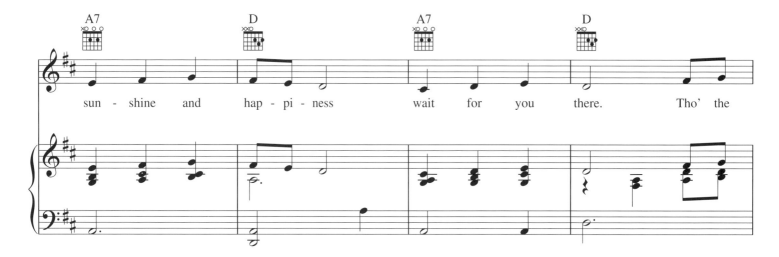

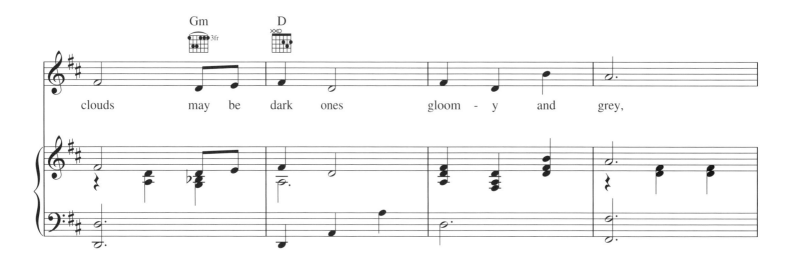

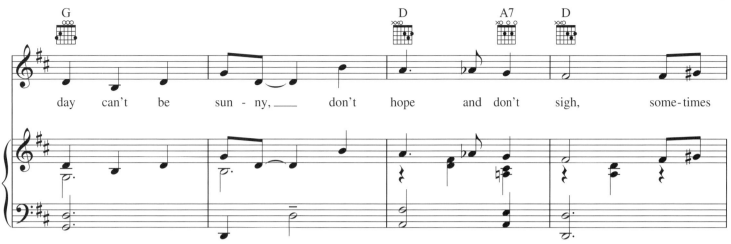

day can't be sun - ny, ____ don't hope and don't sigh, some-times

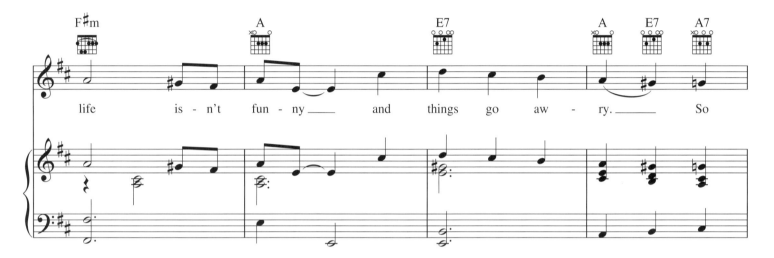

life is - n't fun - ny ____ and things go aw - ry. ____ So

don't be down-heart-ed, stop griev - ing my friend, joy for

you there'll sure - ly be at the rain-bow's end. At the end.

rit.

THE BALLY McQUILTY BAND

Words and Music by
MIKE NONO

March tempo

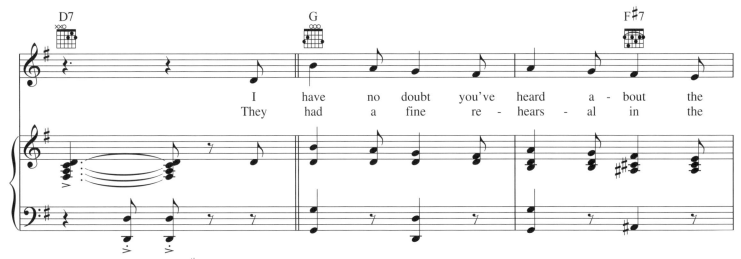

I have no doubt you've heard a - bout the
They had a fine re - hears - al in the

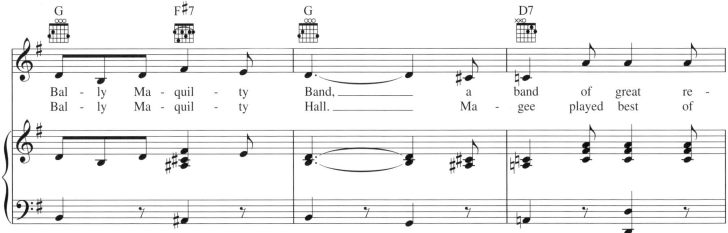

Bal - ly Ma - quil - ty Band, _____ a band of great re -
Bal - ly Ma - quil - ty Hall. _____ Ma - gee played best of

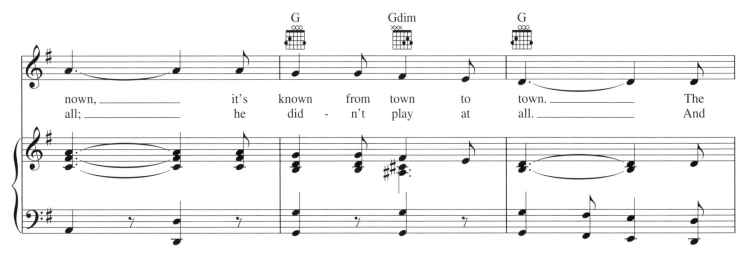

nown, _____ it's known from town to town. _____ The
all; _____ he did - n't play at all. _____ And

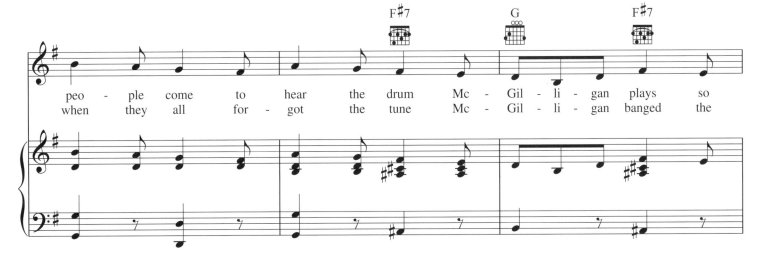

peo - ple come to hear the drum Mc - Gil - li - gan plays so
when they all for - got the tune Mc - Gil - li - gan banged the

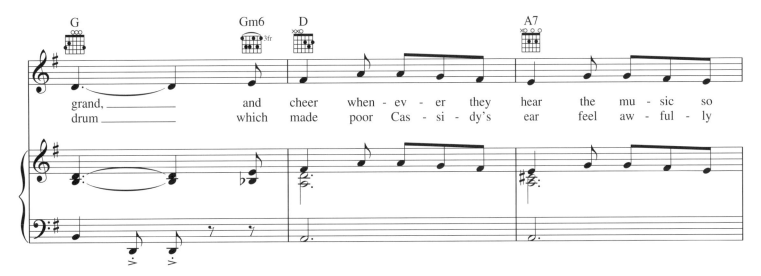

grand, _____ and cheer when - ev - er they hear the mu - sic so
drum _____ which made when poor Cas - si - dy's ear feel aw - ful - ly

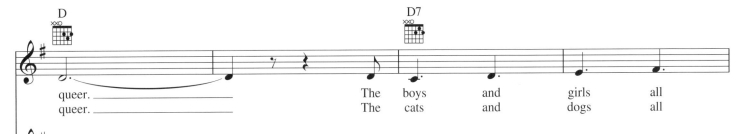

queer. _____ The boys and girls all
queer. _____ The cats and dogs all

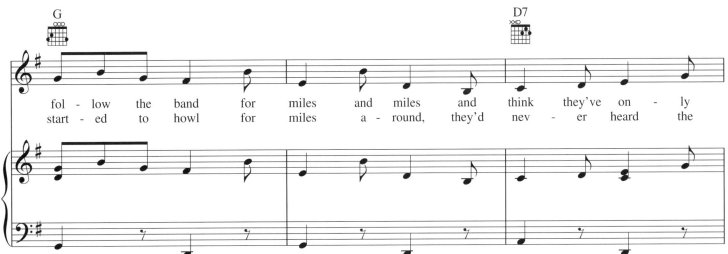

fol - low the band for miles and miles and think they've on - ly
start - ed to howl for miles a - round, they'd nev - er heard the

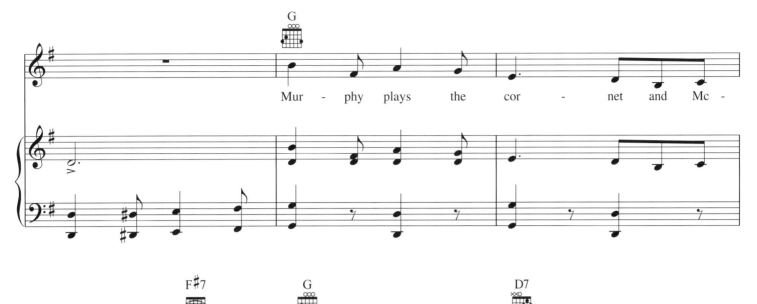

Mur - phy plays the cor - net and Mc -

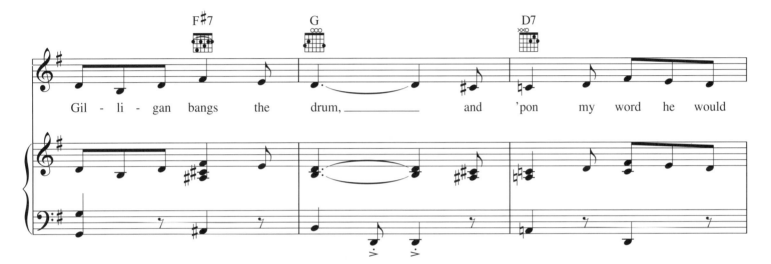

Gil - li - gan bangs the drum, _____ and 'pon my word he would

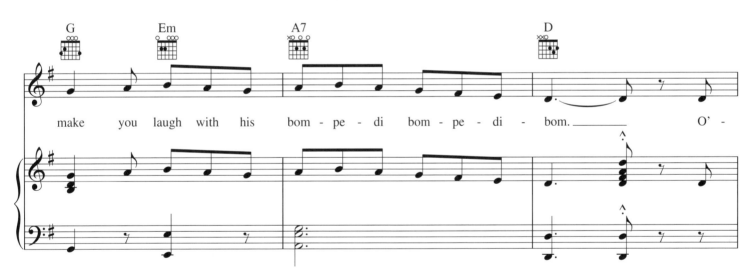

make you laugh with his bom - pe - di bom - pe - di - bom. _____ O' -

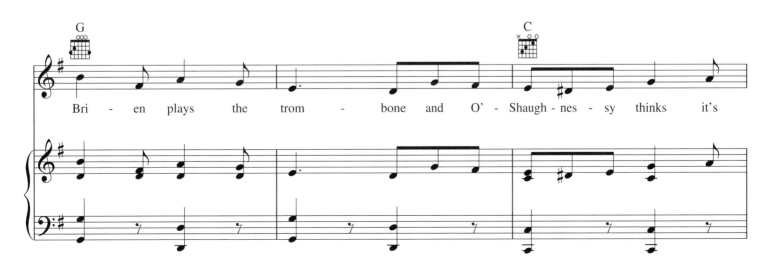

Bri - en plays the trom - bone and O' - Shaugh - nes - sy thinks it's

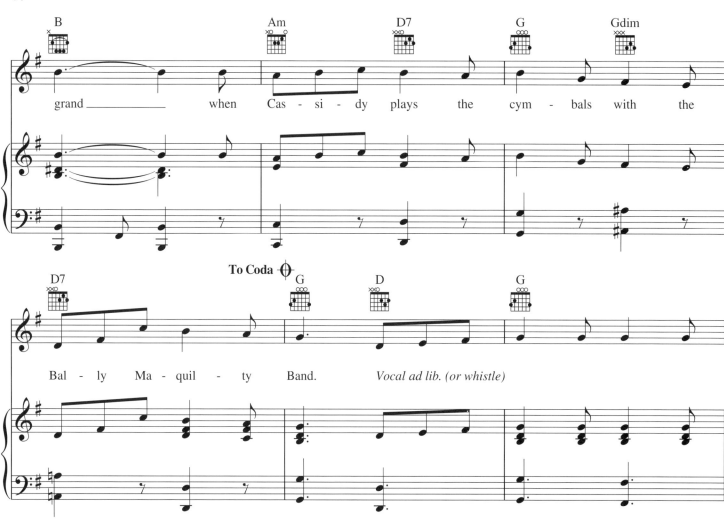

grand _____ when Cas - si - dy plays the cym - bals with the

To Coda

Bal - ly Ma - quil - ty Band. *Vocal ad lib. (or whistle)*

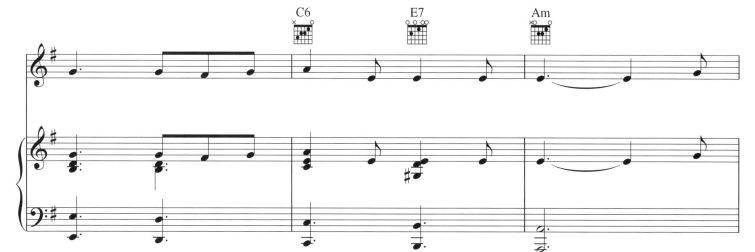

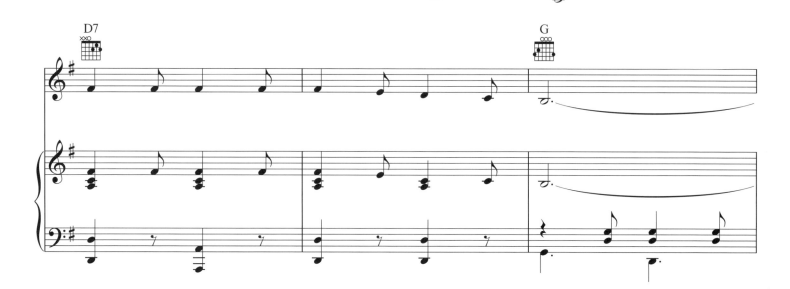

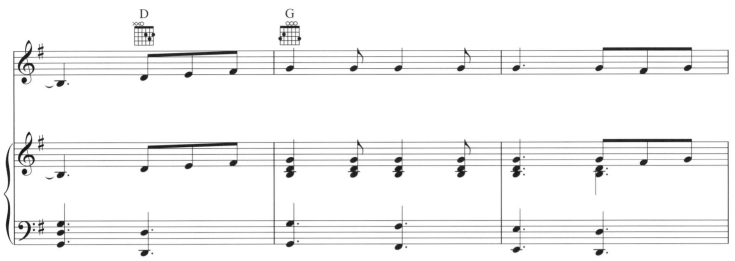

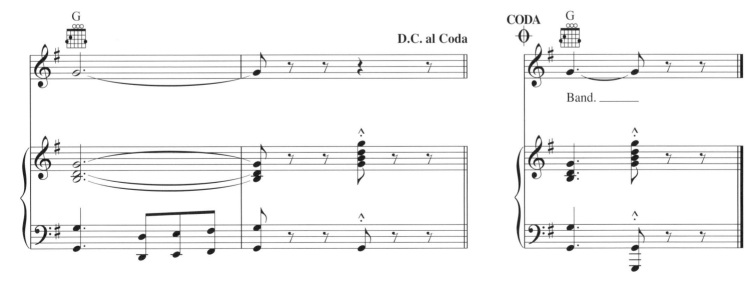

CONNEMARA CRADLE SONG

Words and Music by
DELIA MURPHY

Andante tranquillo

1. On wings of the

wind o'er the dark roll - ing deep,_____ An - gels are
night may your fu - ry be crossed,_____ may no one that's
sail - ing way out in the blue,_____ la - den with
mor - row will stand on the shore,_____ and dad - dy goes

com - ing to watch o'er thy sleep,_____ an - gels are
dear to our is - land be lost._____ Blow the wind
her - rin' of sil - ver - y hue,_____ sil - ver the
sail - ing, a sail - ing no more._____ The nets will be

com - ing to watch o - ver thee, _____ so list to the wind com - ing o - ver the
gen - tly, calm be the foam, _____ shine the light bright - ly to guide them
her - rin' and sil - ver the sea, _____ and soon there'll be sil - ver for ba - by and
dry - ing, the nets heav - en blessed, _____ and safe in my arms, dear, con - tent-ed he'll

sea. _____
home. _____
me. _____
rest. _____

Hear the wind blow, dear, hear the wind blow, _____ lean your head

o - ver and hear the wind blow. _____

2. Oh winds of the
3. The Cur - rachs are blow.
4. The Cur - rachs to -

rit. **p**

COORTIN' IN THE KITCHEN

Words and Music by DELIA MURPHY
Arranged by P.J. RYAN

Brightly, with fire

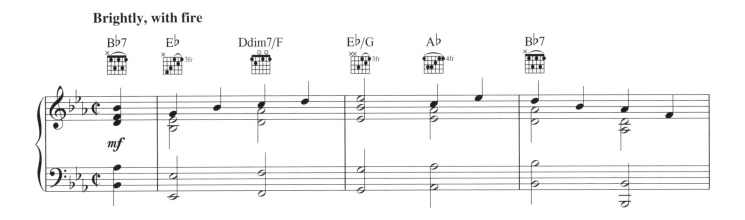

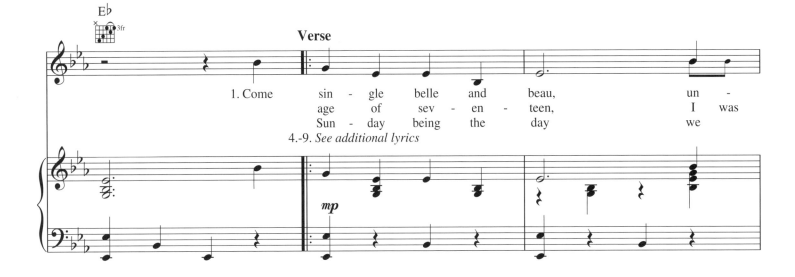

Verse

1. Come sin - gle belle and beau, un -
   age of sev - en - teen, I was
   Sun - day being the day we

4.-9. See additional lyrics

to me pay at - ten - tion, don't ev - er fall in
'pren - ticed to a gro - cer, not far from Ste - phen's
were to have the flare up, I dressed me - self quite

Additional Lyrics

4. Just as the clock struck six we sat down to the table,
   She handed tea and cake and I ate while I was able;
   I drank hot punch and tea till me sides had got a stitch in
   And the hours passed quick away with the coortin' in the kitchen.
   Refrain

5. With me arms around her waist she slyly hinted marriage,
   To the door in dreadful haste came Captain Kelly's carriage;
   Her eyes soon filled with hate and poison she was spitting,
   When the Captain at the door walked straight into the kitchen.
   Refrain

6. She flew up off my knees, full five feet up or higher,
   And over head and heels, threw me slap into the fire;
   My new Repealer's coat, that I bought from Mr. Mitchell,
   With a tweny shilling note, went to blazes in the kitchen.
   Refrain

7. I grieved to see my duds, all smeared with sut and ashes,
   When a tub of dirty suds, right in my face she dashes;
   As I lay on the floor, and the water she kept pitchin',
   The footman broke the door, and marched down into the kitchen.
   Refrain

8. When the captain came down stairs, tho' he saw my situation,
   In spite of all my prayers, I was marched off to the station;
   For me they'd take no bail, tho' to get home I was itchin',
   But I had to tell the tale, how I came into the kitchen.
   Refrain

9. I said she did invite me but she gave a flat denial,
   For assault she did indict me and I was sent for trial;
   She swore I robbed the house in spite of all her screechin'
   And I got six months hard for me coortin' in the kitchen.
   Refrain

DAN O'HARA

Words and Music by
DELIA MURPHY

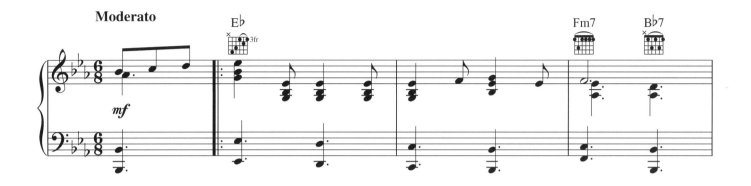

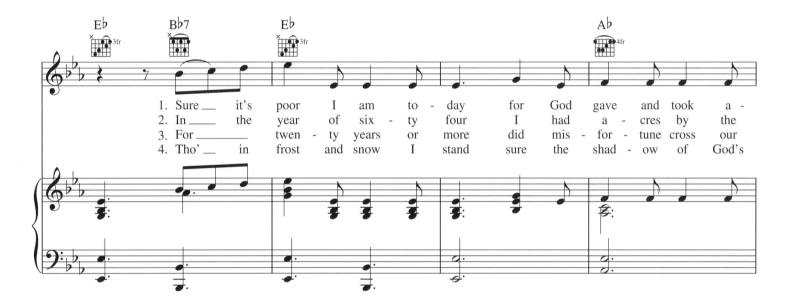

1. Sure ___ it's poor I am to-day for God gave and took a-
2. In ___ the year of six-ty four I had a-cres by the
3. For ___ twen-ty years or more did mis-for-tune cross our
4. Tho' ___ in frost and snow I stand sure the shad-ow of God's

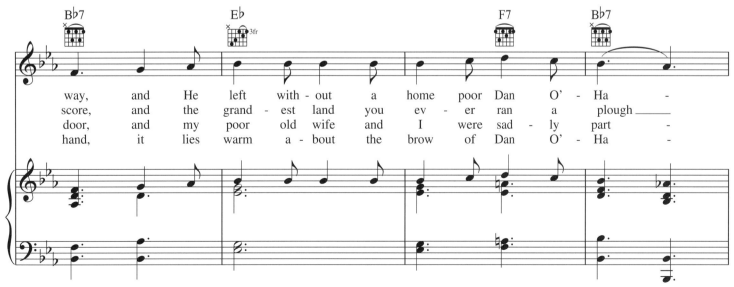

way, and He left with-out a home poor Dan O'-Ha-
score, and the grand-est land you ev-er ran a plough ____
door, and my poor old wife and I were sad-ly part-
hand, it lies warm a-bout the brow of Dan O'-Ha-

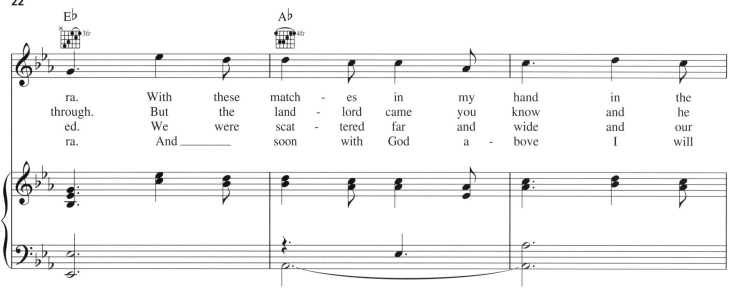

ra. With these match - es in my hand in the
through. But the land - lord came you know and he
ed. We were scat - tered far and wide and our
ra. And _____ soon with God a - bove I will

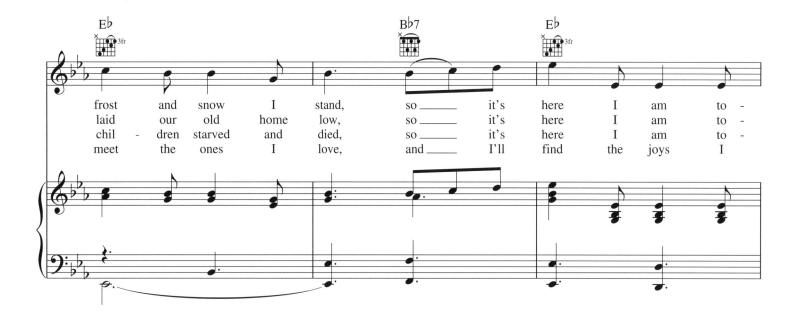

frost and snow I stand, so _____ it's here I am to -
laid our old home low, so _____ it's here I am to -
chil - dren starved and died, so _____ it's here I am to -
meet the ones I love, and _____ I'll find the joys I

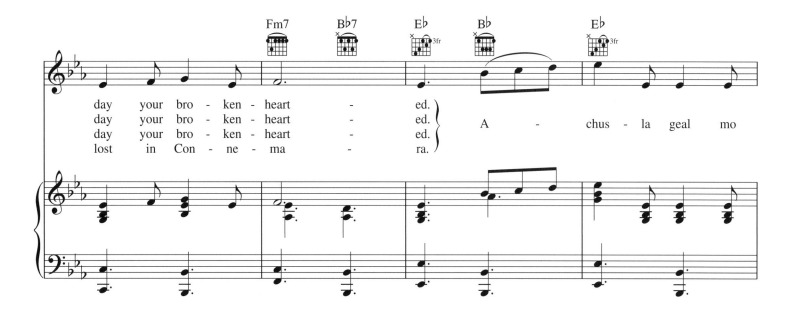

day your bro - ken - heart - ed.
day your bro - ken - heart - ed.
day your bro - ken - heart - ed.
lost in Con - ne - ma - ra.

A - chus - la geal mo

chree, won't you buy a box from me, and you'll have the prayers of

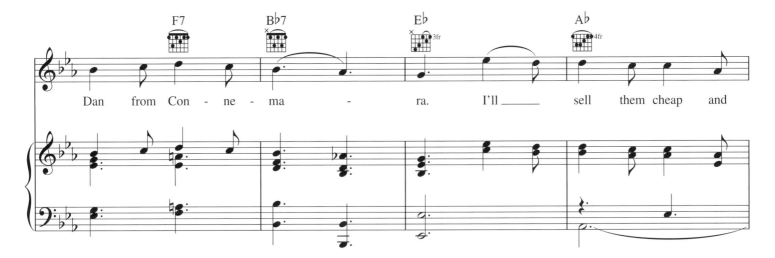

Dan from Con - ne - ma - ra. I'll _____ sell them cheap and

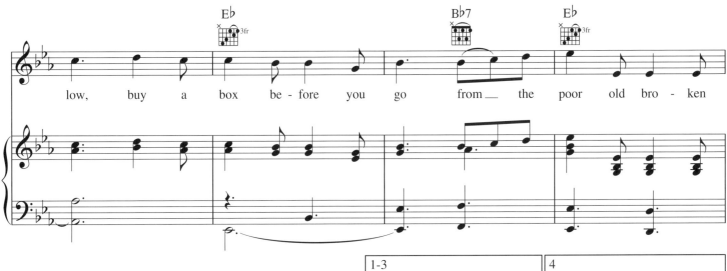

low, buy a box be - fore you go from ___ the poor old bro - ken

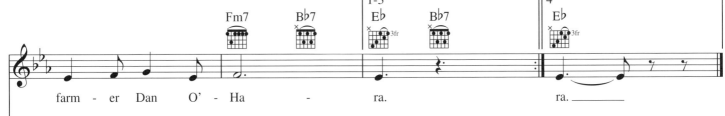

farm - er Dan O' - Ha - ra. ra. _____

DEAR OLD DONEGAL

Words and Music by
STEVE GRAHAM

seems like on-ly yes-ter-day, I sailed from out of Cork, _____ a
give a par-ty when I go home, they'll come from near and far, _____ they'll

wan-der-er from Er-in's isle, I land-ed in New York. _____ There
line the roads for miles and miles, with I-rish jaunt-in' cars. _____ The

was-n't a soul ___ to greet me there, a stran - ger on your shore, ___ but
spir - its - 'll flow ___ and we'll be gay, we'll fill your hearts with joy, ___ the

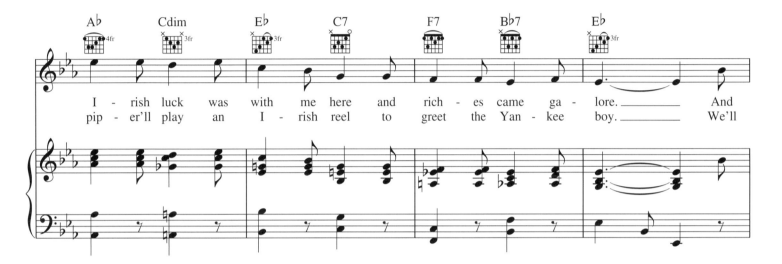

I - rish luck was with me here and rich - es came ga - lore. ___ And
pip - er'll play an I - rish reel to greet the Yan - kee boy. ___ We'll

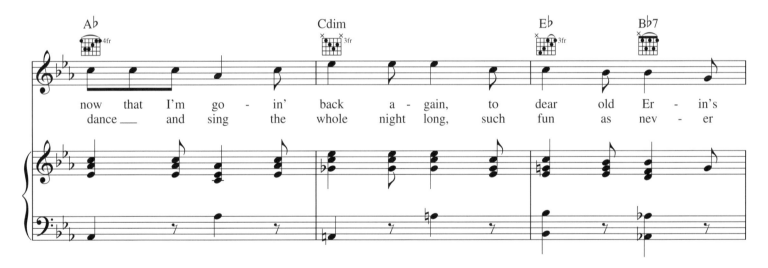

now that I'm go - in' back a - gain, to dear old Er - in's
dance ___ and sing the whole night long, such fun as nev - er

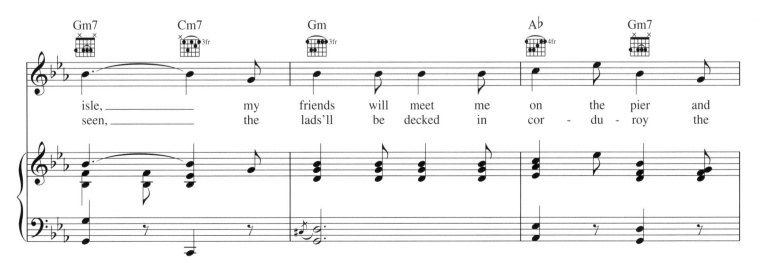

isle, ___ my friends will meet me on the pier and
seen, ___ the lads'll be decked in cor - du - roy the

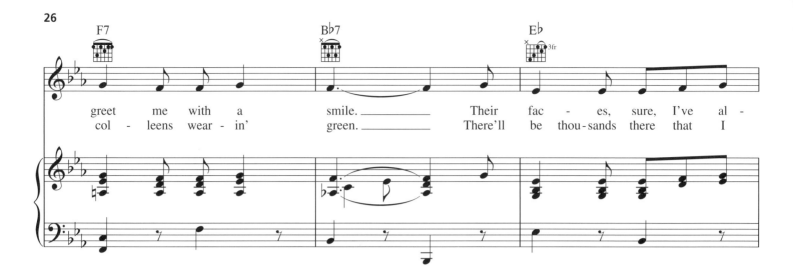

greet me with a smile. _____ Their fac - es, sure, I've al -
col - leens wear - in' green. _____ There'll be thou - sands there that I

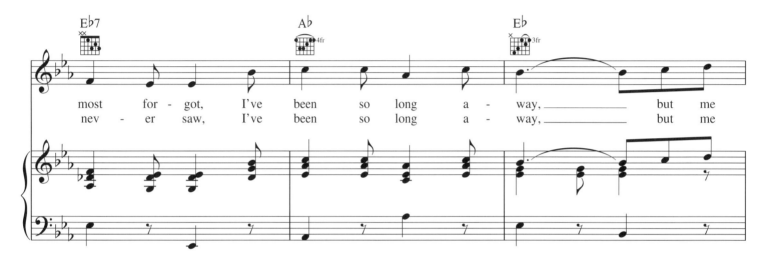

most for - got, I've been so long a - way, _____ but me
nev - er saw, I've been so long a - way, _____ but me

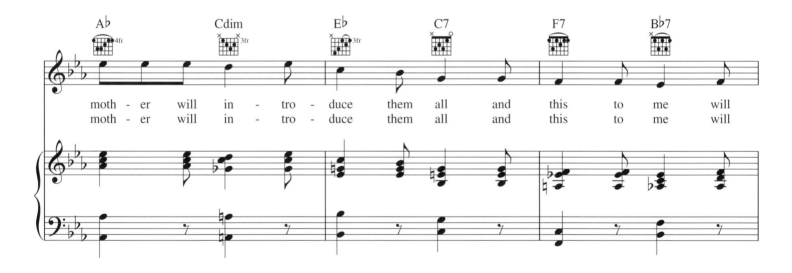

moth - er will in - tro - duce them all and this to me will
moth - er will in - tro - duce them all and this to me will

say: _____ } Shake hands with your Un - cle Mike, me boy, and
say: _____ }

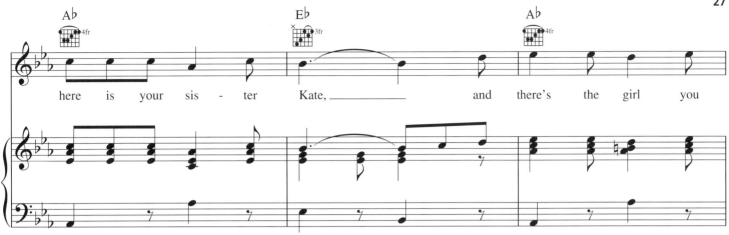

here is your sis - ter Kate, _____ and there's the girl you

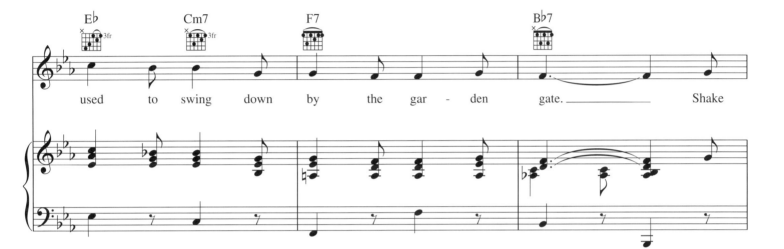

used to swing down by the gar - den gate. _____ Shake

hands with all of the neigh - bors _____ and kiss the col - leens

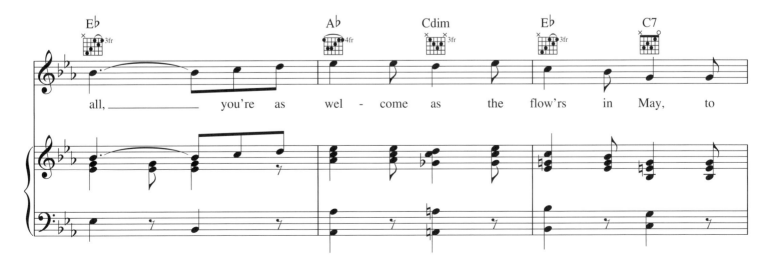

all, _____ you're as wel - come as the flow'rs in May, to

28

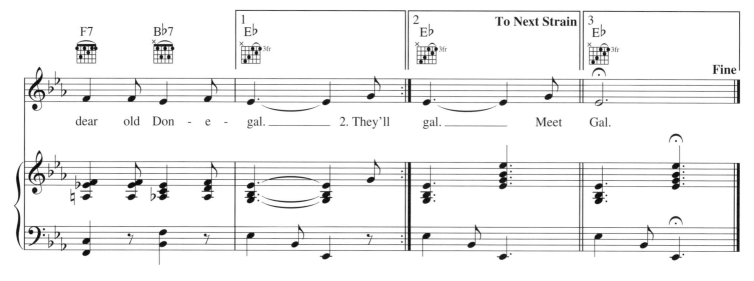

DOWN BY THE GLENSIDE

Words and Music by PETER KEARNEY
and PATRICK RYAN

Moderately, with much expression

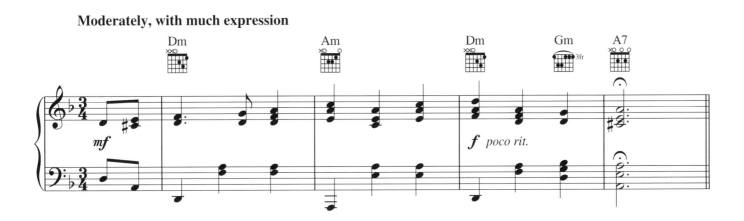

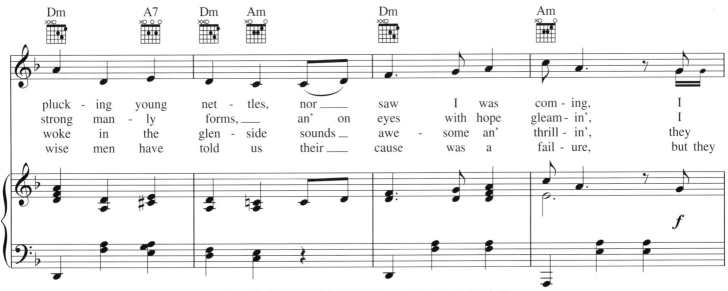

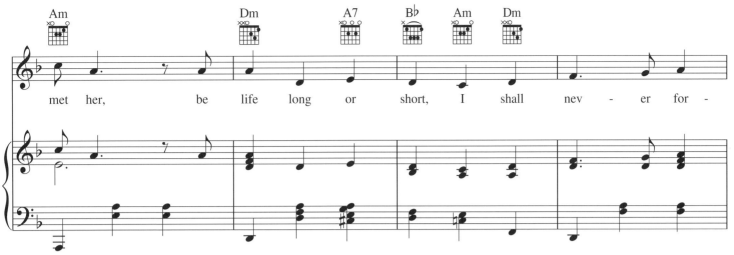

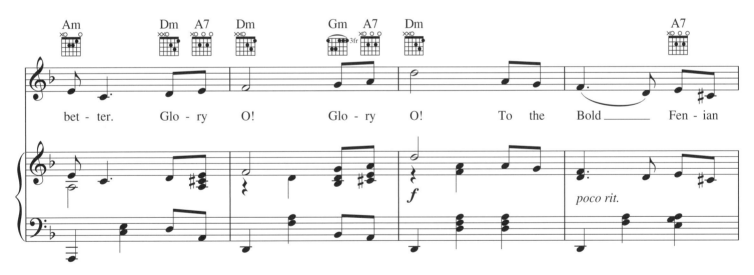

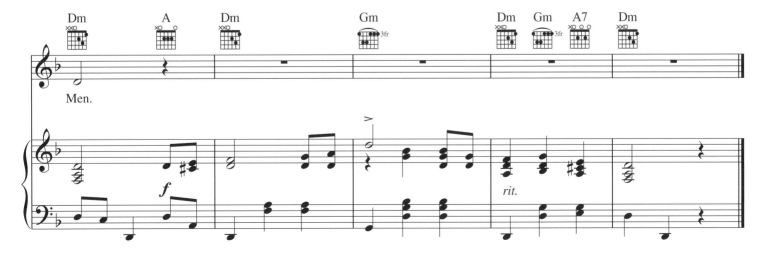

GALWAY BAY

By DR. ARTHUR COLAHAN

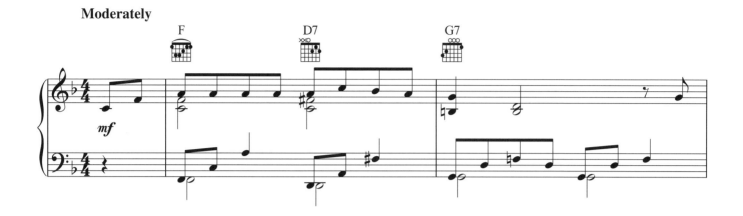

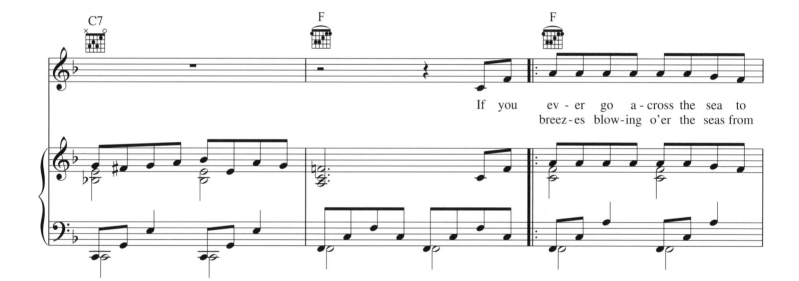

star. And if there is going to be a life here - af - ter, and

some-how I am sure there's going to be, I will ask my God to let me make my

heav - en in that dear land a - cross the I - rish sea.

GARDEN WHERE
THE PRATIES GROW

Words and Music by
JOHNNY PATTERSON

Moderately, with feeling

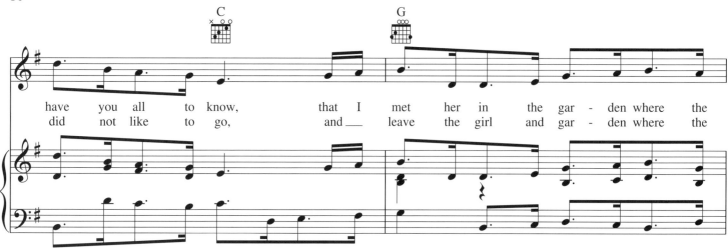

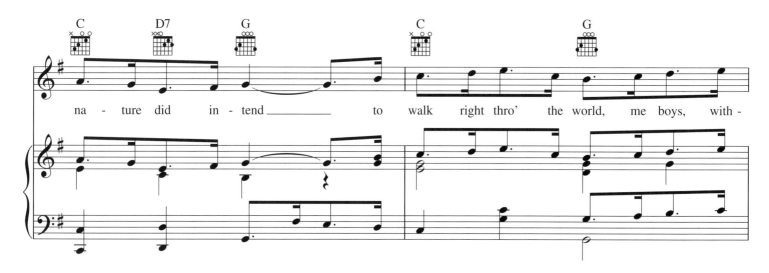

have you all to know that I met her in the gar - den where the pra - ties grow.

2. She was
3. Says I,
4. Says I,
5. Now her

Additional Lyrics

3. Says I, "My lovely colleen,
   I hope you'll pardon me,"
   But she wasn't like those city girls
   Who'd say "you're making free,"
   She answered then right modestly,
   And curtsied very low,
   Saying, "You're welcome to the garden
   Where the praties grow."

4. Says I, "My lovely darling,
   I'm tired of single life.
   And if you've no objections,
   I'll make you my sweet wife."
   Says she, "I'll ask my parents,
   If you'll meet me in the garden
   Where the praties grow."

5. Now her parents they consented,
   And we're blessed with children three,
   Two girls just like their mother,
   And a boy the image of me;
   We'll train them up in decency
   The way they ought to go;
   But I'll ne'er forget the garden
   Where the praties grow.

HANNIGAN'S HOOLEY
(Come Into the Parlour)

Words and Music by
CECIL SHERIDAN

Brightly

Now Han-ni-gan was as I-rish-man who came from E-rin's Isle, _____ he was a rogue who had a brogue you'd hear for half a mile. _____ When Han-ni-gan gives a hoo-ley sure the news soon gets a-

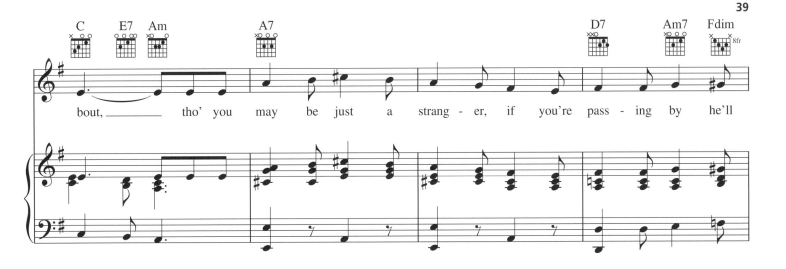

bout, _____ tho' you may be just a strang - er, if you're pass - ing by he'll

shout, Oh! Come in - to the par - lour you can make your - self at

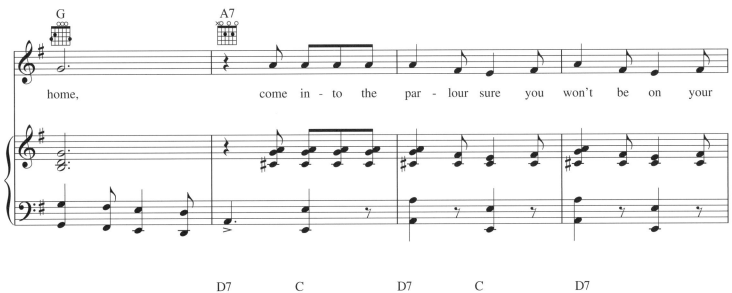

home, come in - to the par - lour sure you won't be on your

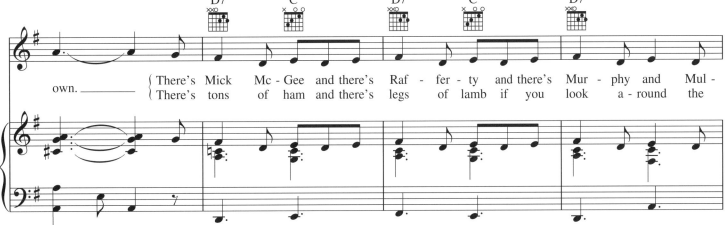

own. _____
There's Mick Mc - Gee and there's Raf - fer - ty and there's Mur - phy and Mul -
There's tons of ham and there's legs of lamb if you look a - round the

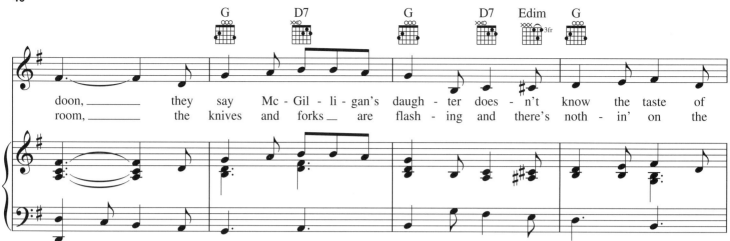

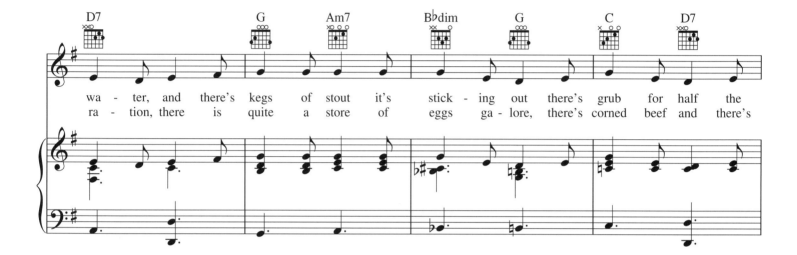

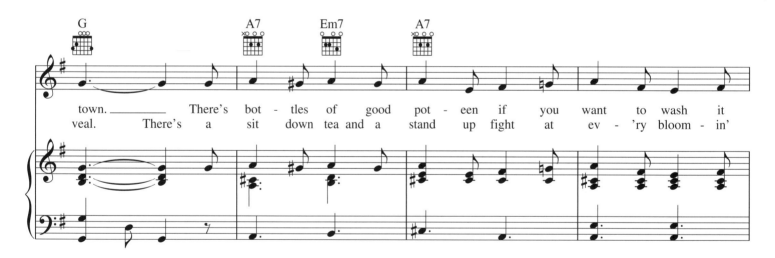

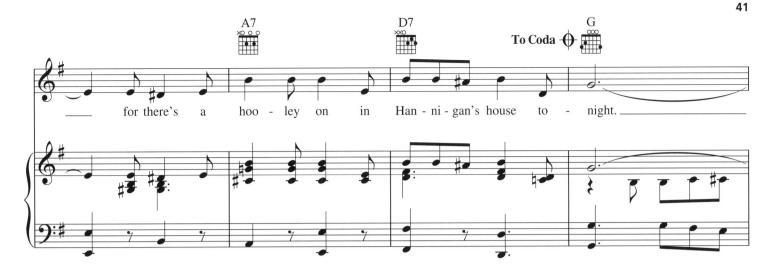

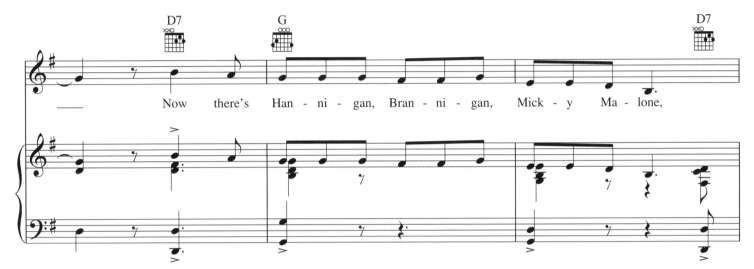

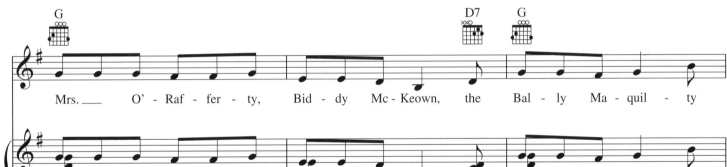

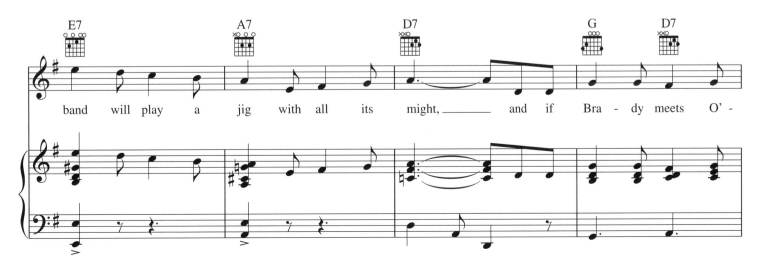

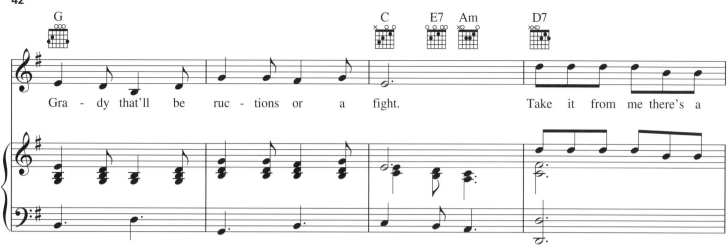

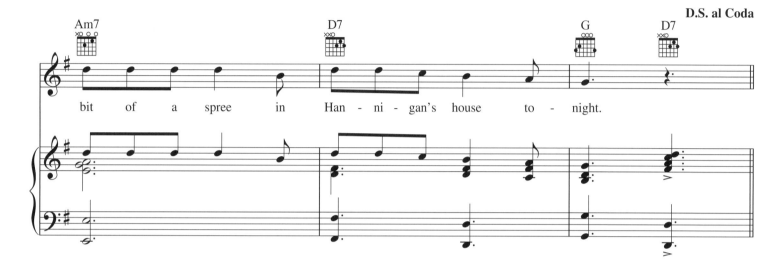

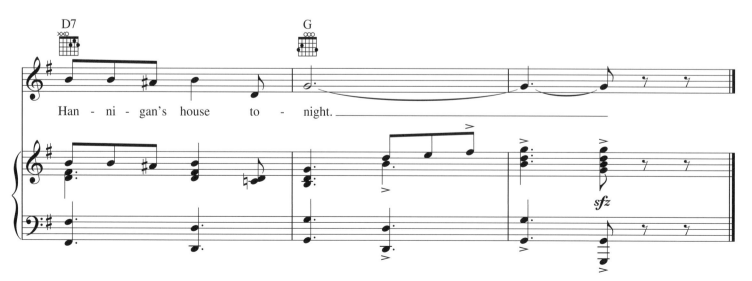

HELLO, PATSY FAGAN
(The Dacent Irish Boy)

Words and Music by
T.P. KEENAN

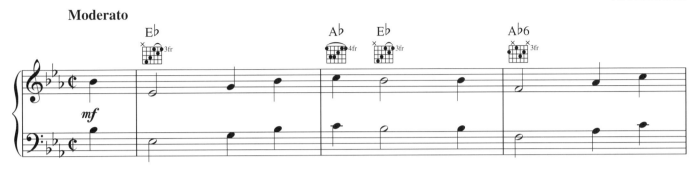

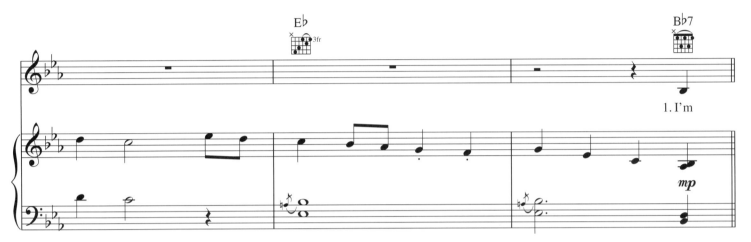

1. I'm

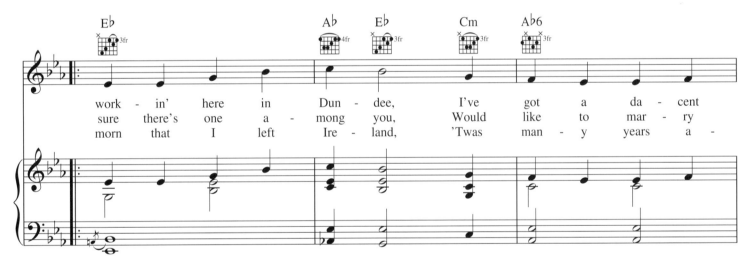

work - in' here in Dun - dee, I've got a da - cent
sure there's one a - mong you, Would like to mar - ry
morn that I left Ire - land, 'Twas man - y years a -

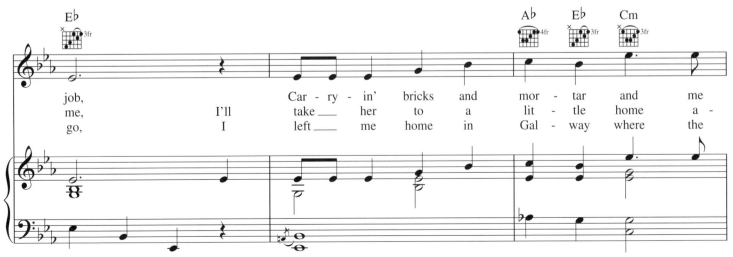

job, Car - ry - in' bricks and mor - tar and me
me, I'll take ___ her to a lit - tle home a -
go, I left ___ me home in Gal - way where the

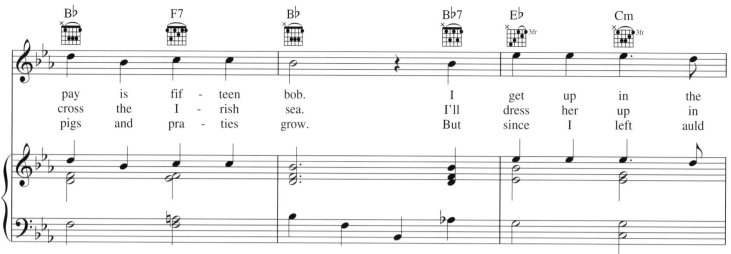

pay   is   fif - teen   bob.   I   get   up   in   the
cross the   I - rish   sea.   I'll   dress her   up   in
pigs   and   pra - ties   grow.   But   since I   left auld

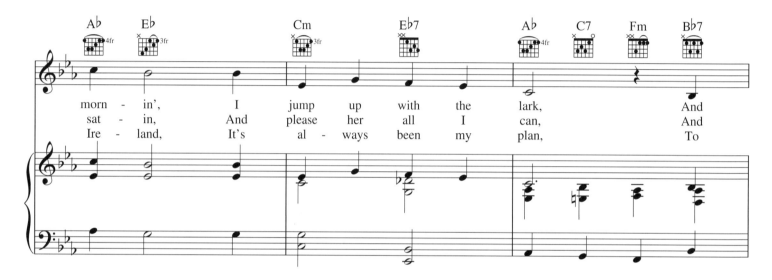

morn - in',   I   jump   up   with   the   lark,   And
sat - in,   And   please her   all   I   can,   And
Ire - land,   It's   al -   ways been   my   plan,   To

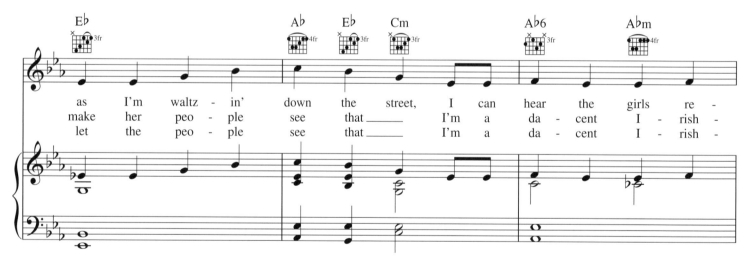

as   I'm   waltz - in'   down   the   street, I   can   hear   the   girls   re -
make her   peo - ple   see   that_____   I'm a   da -   cent I -   rish -
let   the   peo - ple   see   that_____   I'm a   da -   cent I -   rish -

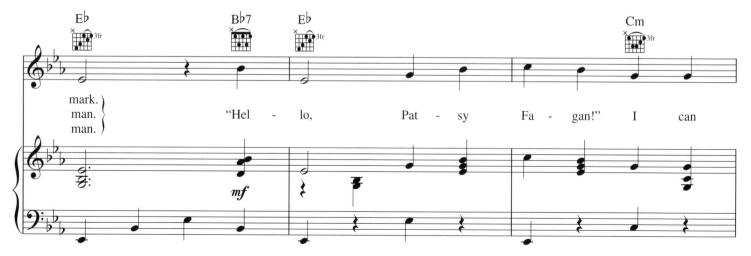

mark. }
man. }
man. }   "Hel - lo,   Pat - sy   Fa - gan!"   I   can

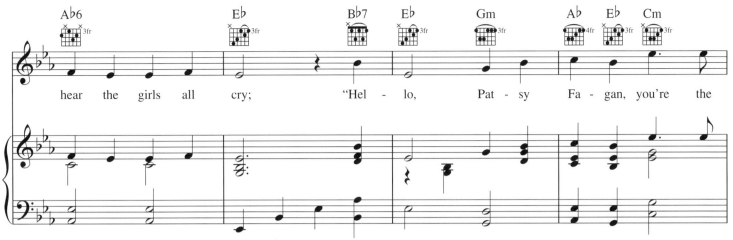

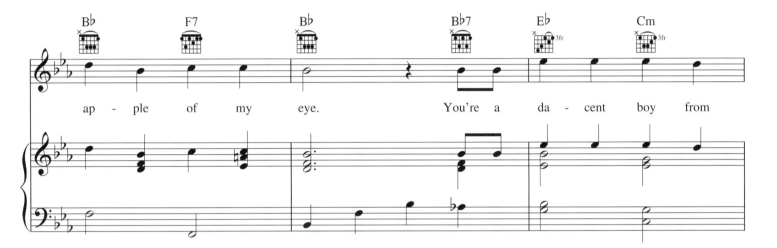

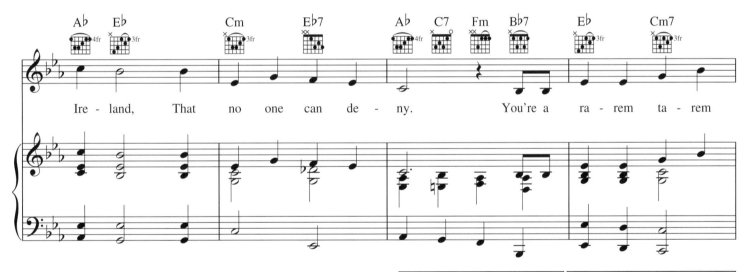

HOMES OF DONEGAL

Words and Music by
SEAN MacBRIDE

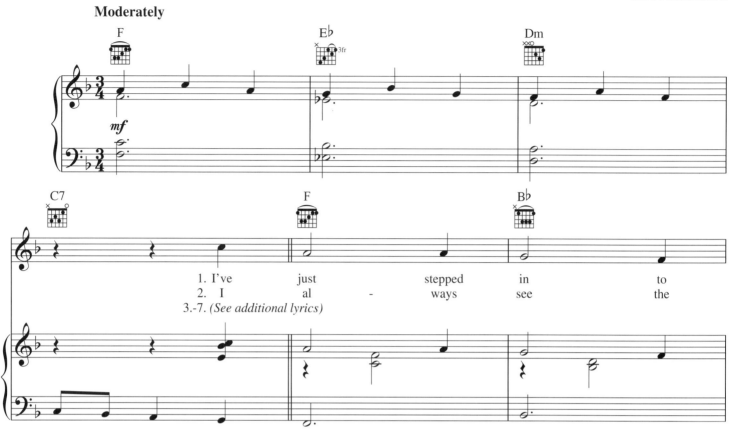

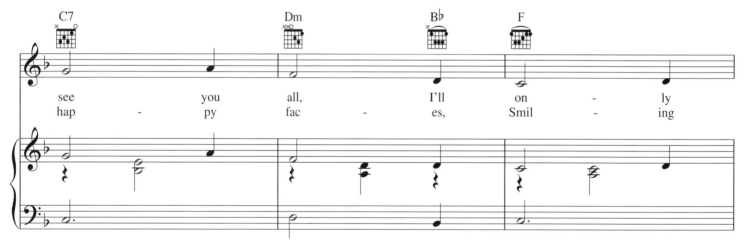

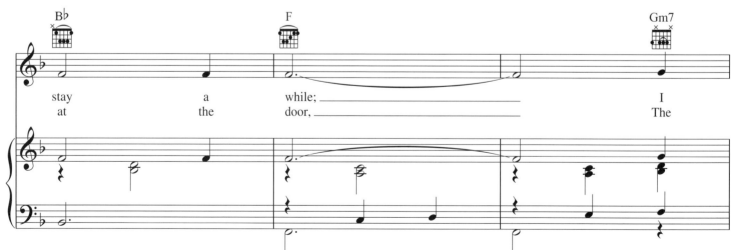

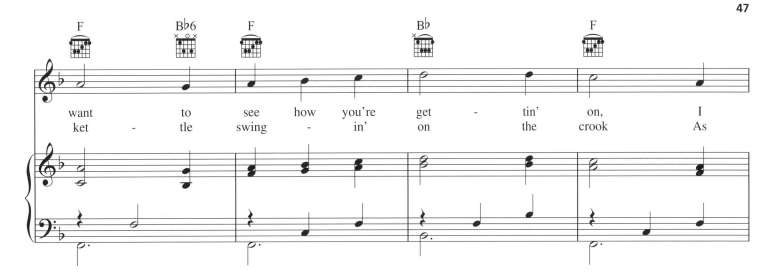

want to see how you're get - tin' on, I
ket - tle swing - in' on the crook As

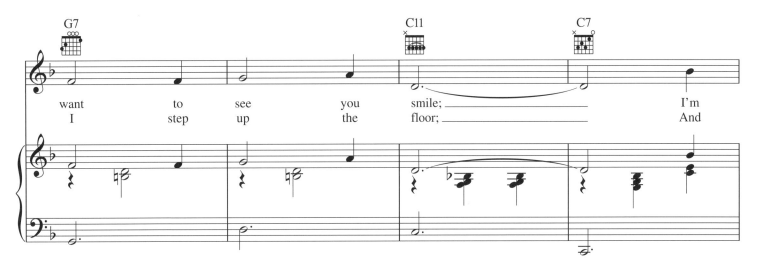

want to see you smile; I'm
I step up the floor; And

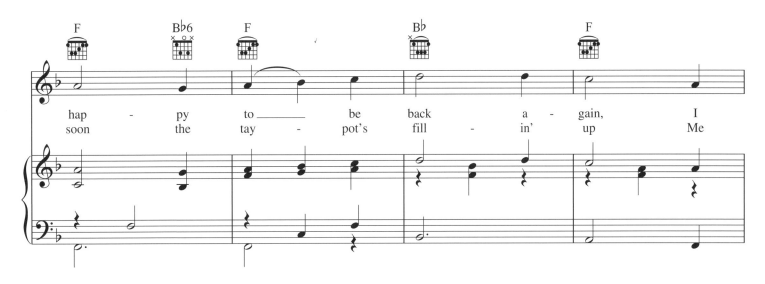

hap - py to be back a - gain, I
soon the tay - pot's fill - in' up Me

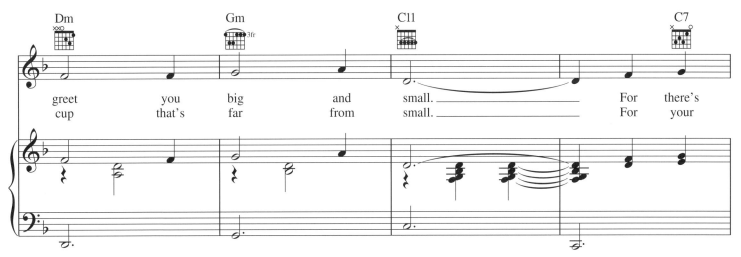

greet you big and small. For there's
cup that's far from small. For your

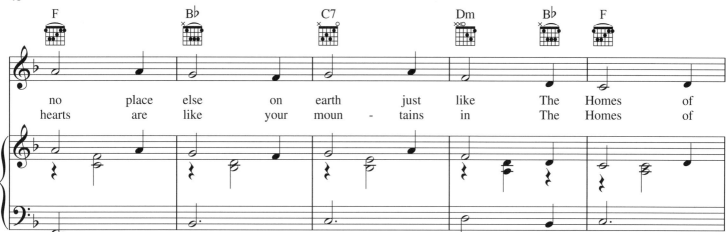

no place else on earth just like The Homes of
hearts are like on your moun - tains like in The Homes of

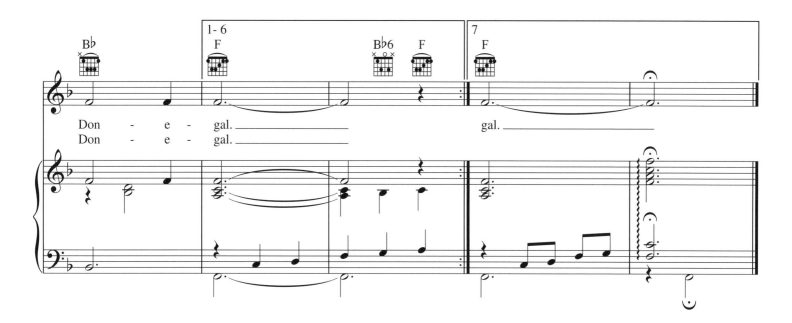

Don - e - gal. _____ gal. _____
Don - e - gal. _____

Additional Lyrics

3. To see your homes at parting day
   Of that I never tire
   And hear the porridge bubblin'
   In a big pot on the fire
   The lamp a-light, the dresser bright
   The big clock on the wall,
   O, a sight serene celestial scene
   In the Homes of Donegal.

4. I long to sit along with you
   And while away the night
   With tales of yore and fairy lore
   Beside your fires so bright
   And then to see prepared to me
   A shake-down by the wall
   There's repose for weary wand'rers
   In the Homes of Donegal.

5. Outside the night winds shriek and howl
   Inside there's peace and calm
   A picture on the wall up there's
   Our Saviour with a lamb
   The hope of wandering sheep like me
   And all who rise and fall
   There's a touch of heavenly love around
   The Homes of Donegal,

6. A tramp I am and a tramp I've been
   A tramp I'll always be
   Me father tramped, me mother tramped
   Sure trampin's bred in me
   If some there are my ways disdain
   And won't have me at all
   Sure I'll always find a welcome
   In the Homes of Donegal.

7. The time has come and I must go
   I bid you all adieu
   The open highway calls me forth
   To do the things I do
   And when I'm trampin' far away
   I'll hear your voices call
   And please God I'll soon return unto
   The Homes of Donegal.

THE ISLE OF INNISFREE

Words and Music by
DICK FARRELY

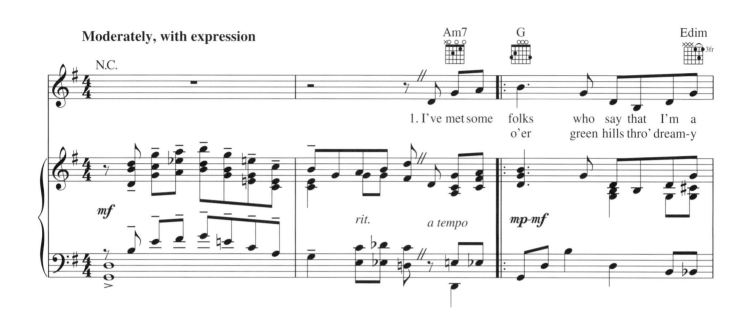

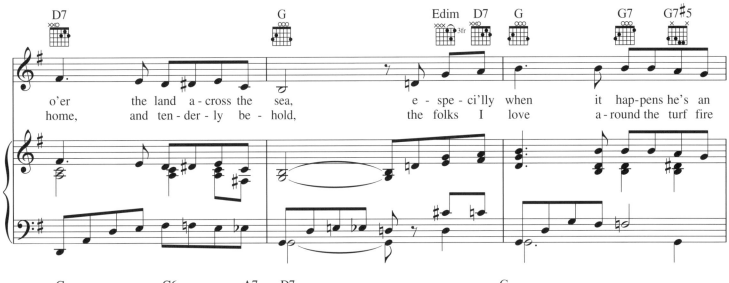

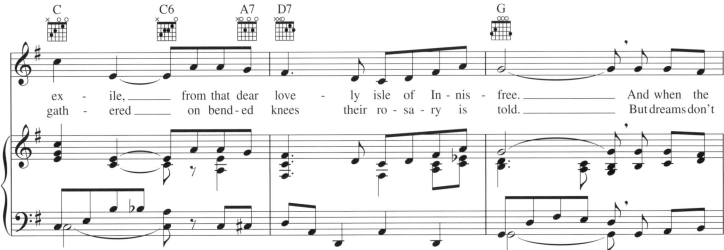

IT'S THE SAME OLD SHILLELAGH

Words and Music by
PAT WHITE

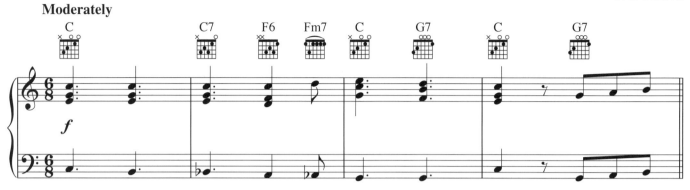

Fif - ty years a - go me fa - ther left old Er - in's
go - in' on the po - lice force, it's the on - ly thing to

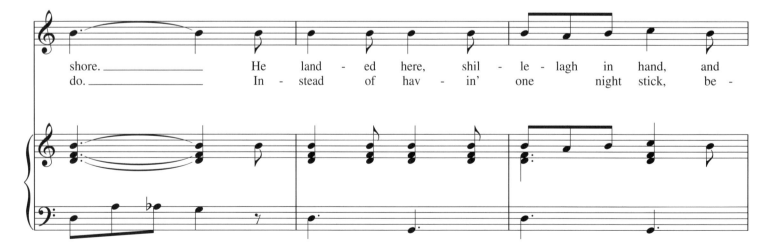

shore. _____ He land - ed here, shil - le - lagh in hand, and
do. _____ In - stead of hav - in' one night stick, be -

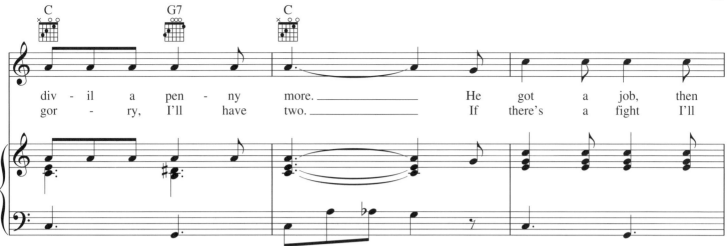

div - il a pen - ny more._____ He got a job, then
gor - ry, I'll have two._____ If there's a fight I'll

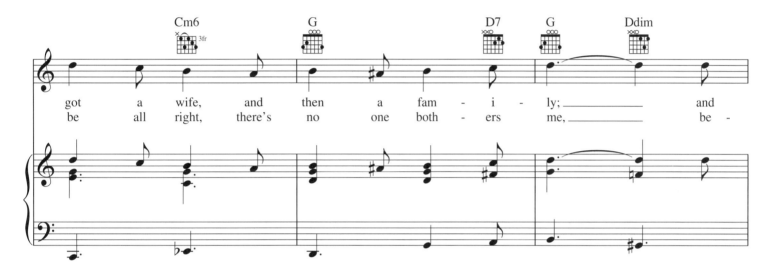

got a wife, and then a fam - i - ly;_____ and
be all right, there's no one both - ers me,_____ be -

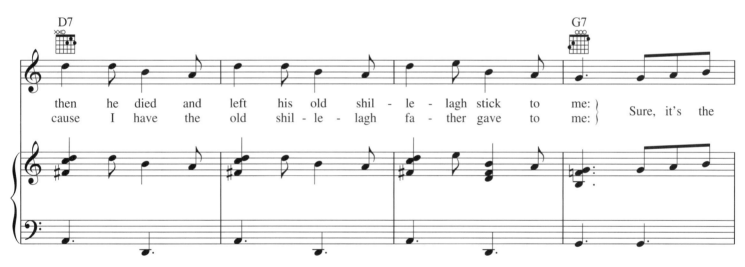

then he died and left his old shil - le - lagh stick to me: }
cause I have the old shil - le - lagh fa - ther gave to me: } Sure, it's the

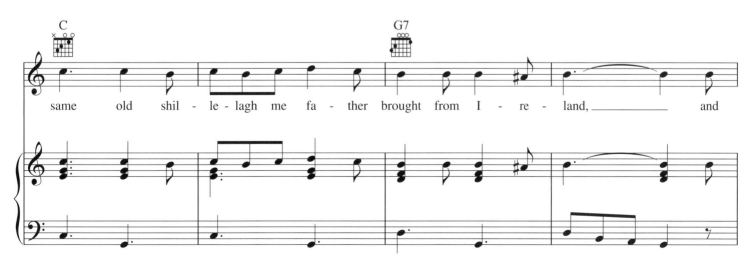

same old shil - le - lagh me fa - ther brought from I - re - land,_____ and

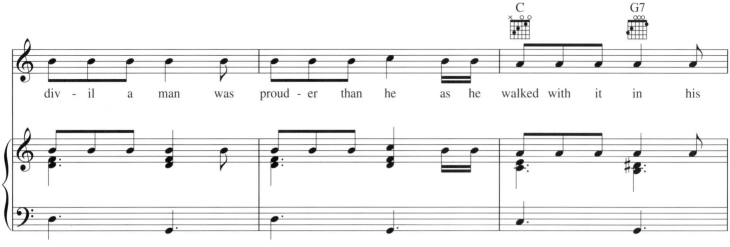

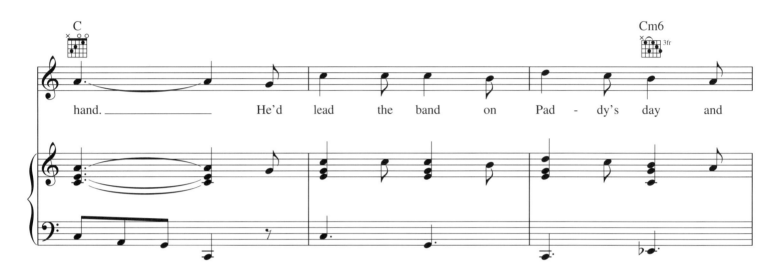

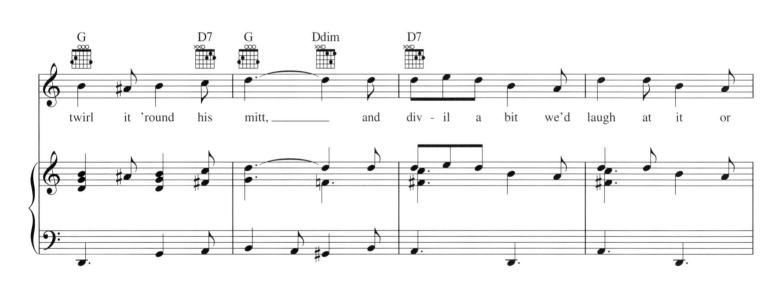

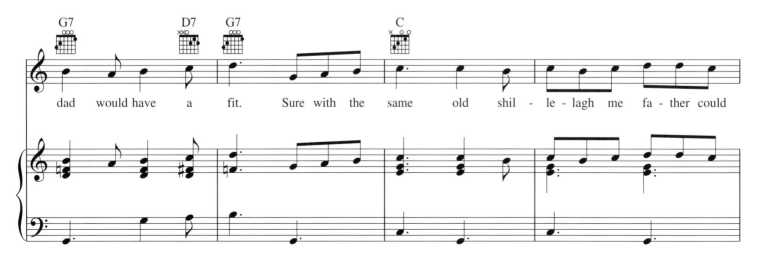

lick a doz - en men. _____ As fast as they'd get up, be - gor - ry, he'd

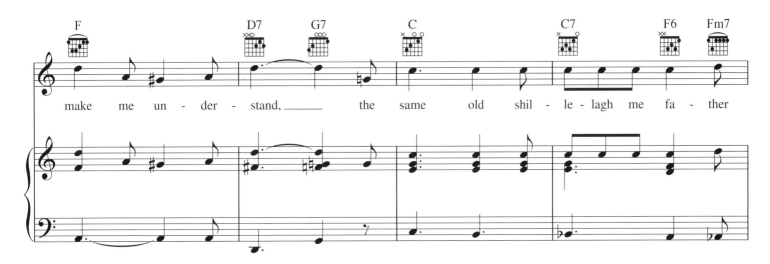

knock 'em down a - gain. _____ And man - y's the time he used it on me to

make me un - der - stand, _____ the same old shil - le - lagh me fa - ther

brought from I - re - land.   I'm   land. _____

THE LITTLE OLD MUD CABIN ON THE HILL

Words and Music Adapted by
S. GAFFNEY

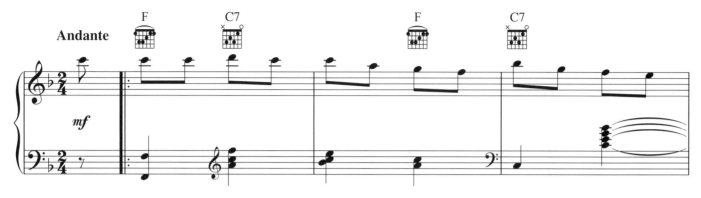

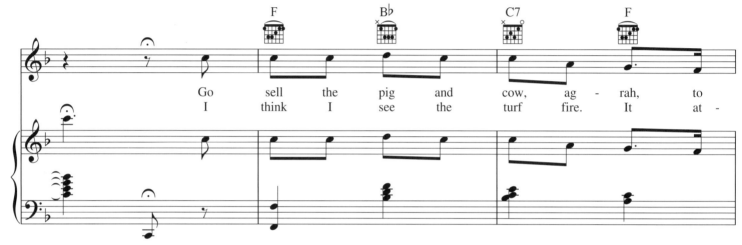

Go sell the pig and cow, ag - rah, to
I think I see the turf fire. It at -

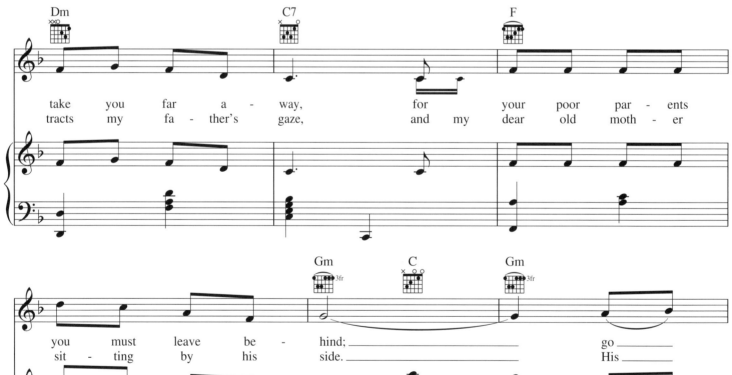

take you far a - way, for your poor par - ents
tracts my fa - ther's gaze, and my dear poor old moth - er

you must leave be - hind; ___ go ___
sit - ting by his side. ___ His ___

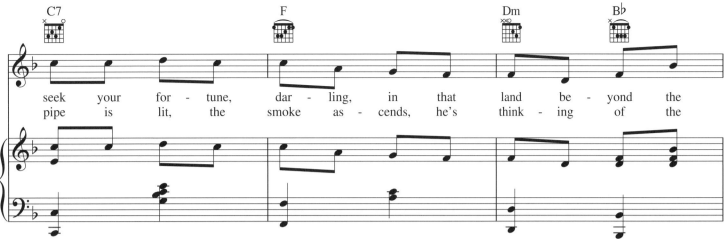

seek your for - tune, dar - ling, in that land be - yond the
pipe is lit, the smoke as - cends, he's think - ing of the

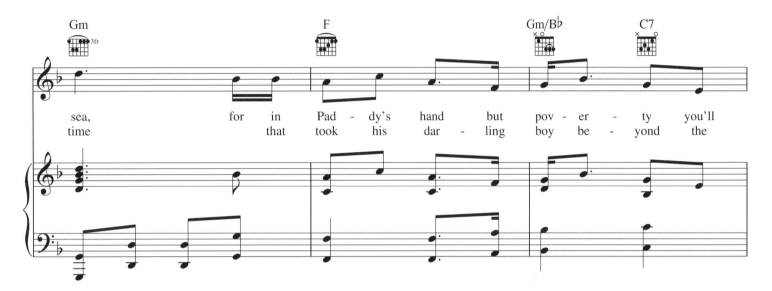

sea, for in Pad - dy's hand but pov - er - ty you'll
time that took his dar - ling boy be - yond the

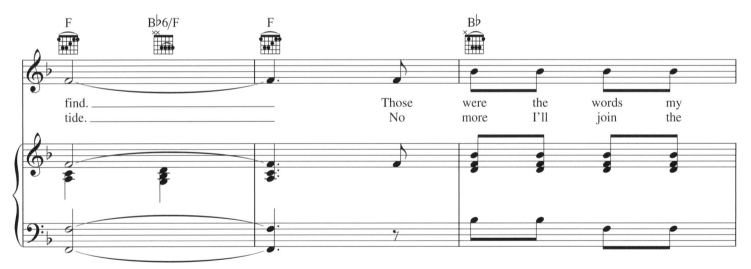

find. _____ Those were the words my
tide. _____ No more I'll join the

fa - ther said when I left old Ire - land, and the
mer - ry dance up - on the cab - in floor, to

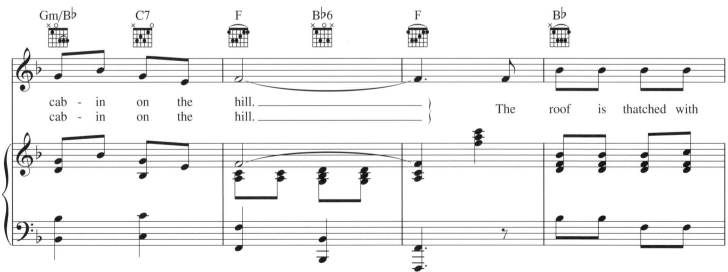

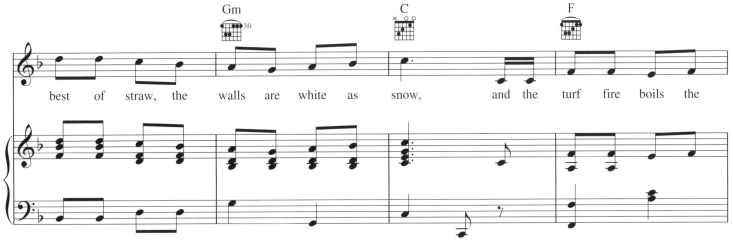

best of straw, the walls are white as snow, and the turf fire boils the

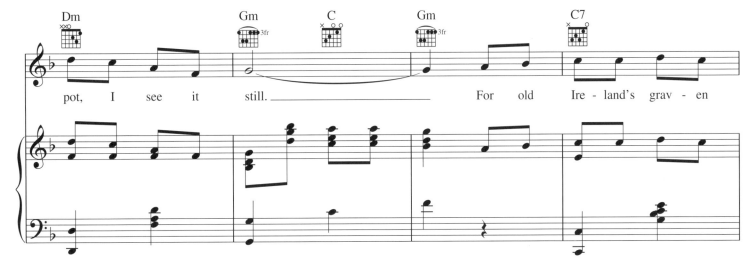

pot, I see it still. _____ For old Ire - land's grav - en

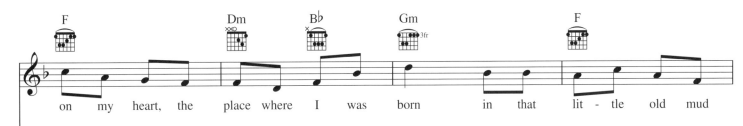

on my heart, the place where I was born in that lit - tle old mud

cab - in on the hill. _____

THE MOONSHINER

Words and Music by DELIA MURPHY
Arranged by P.J. RYAN
and SEAMUS KAVANAGH

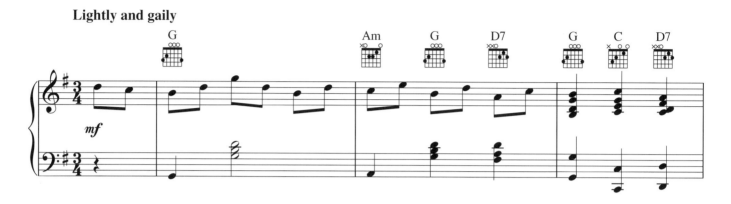

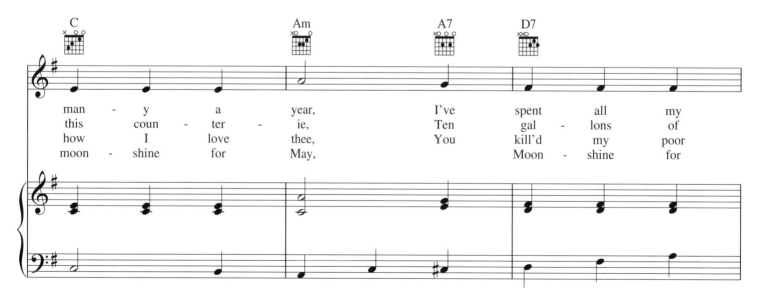

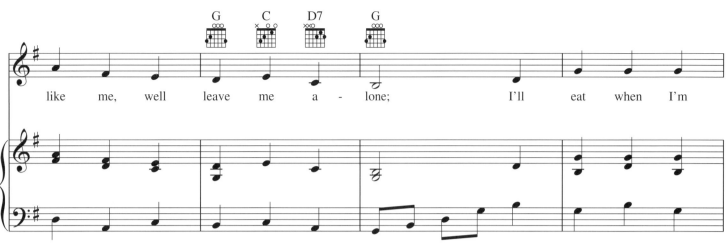

like me, well leave me a - lone; I'll eat when I'm

hun - gry, I'll drink when I'm dry, If _____ moon - shine won't

kill me, I'll live till I die.

2. I'll
3. Moon - die.
4. I'll have

RILEY'S DAUGHTER

Words and Music by
MORTON MORROW

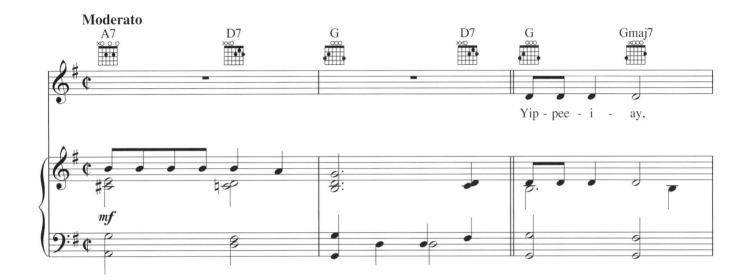

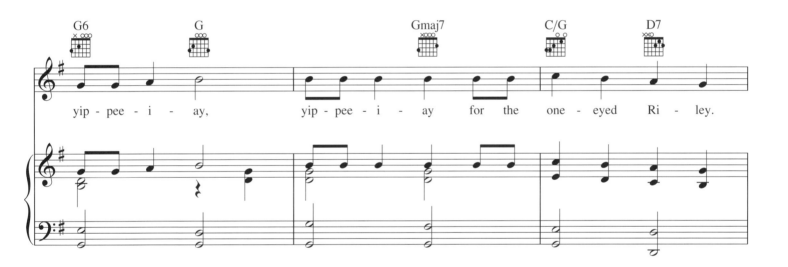

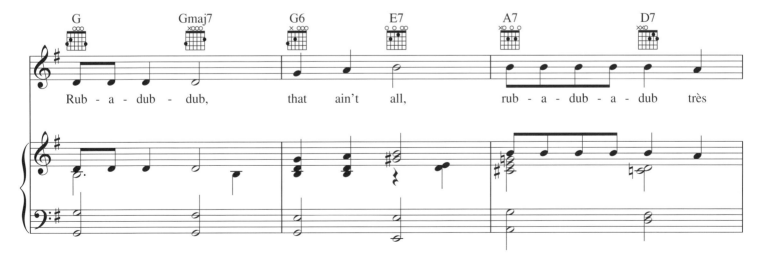

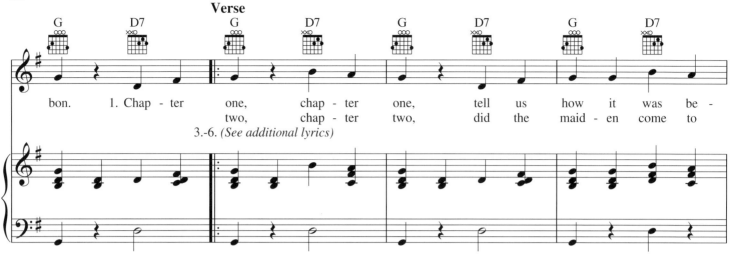

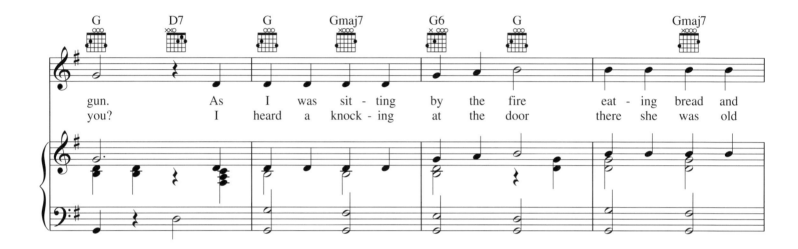

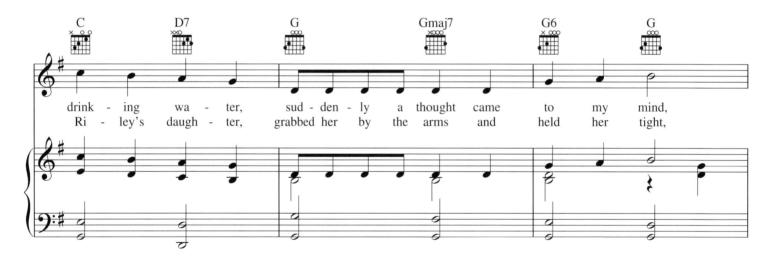

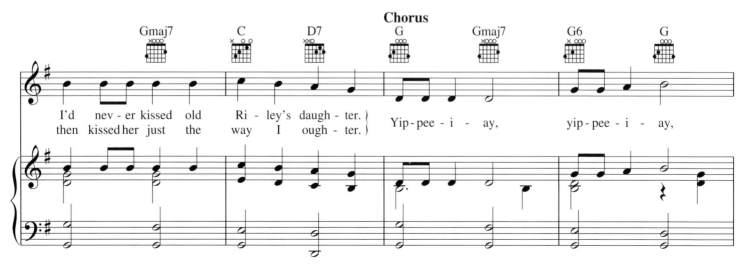

Additional Lyrics

3. Chapter three, chapter three, did she sit upon your knee?
She gave a yell and shouted out
Louder than a railway porter
Never heard the like since I was born
Shoutin' for Pa was Riley's daughter.
Chorus

4. Chapter four, chapter four, did you go and lock the door?
I heard a footstep on the stair
Old man Riley out for slaughter
With a brace of pistols in his hand
After the man who'd kissed his daughter.
Chorus

5. Chapter five, chapter five, how did you get out alive?
I grabbed old Riley by the neck
Pushed his head in a bucket of water
Took those pistols from his hand
Quicker than I had kissed his daughter.
Chorus

6. Chapter six, chapter six, are you still up to your tricks?
And now I'm growing old and grey
And my memory's getting shorter
But until my dying day
I will remember Riley's daughter.
Chorus

THE SPINNING WHEEL

Words and Music by DELIA MURPHY
and JOHN FRANCIS WALLER

Andante con moto

1. Mel - low the moon - light to shine is be - gin - ning,
2.-6. *(See additional lyrics)*

close by the win - dow young Ei - leen is spin - ning;

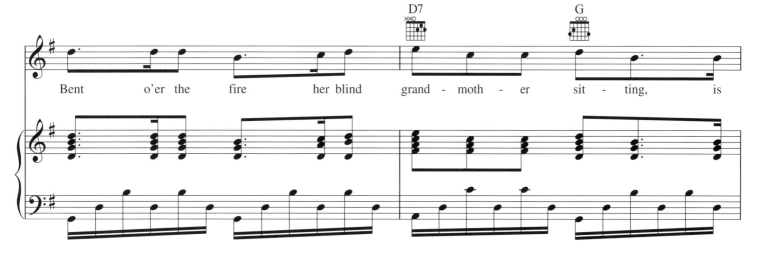

Bent o'er the fire her blind grand-moth-er sit-ting, is

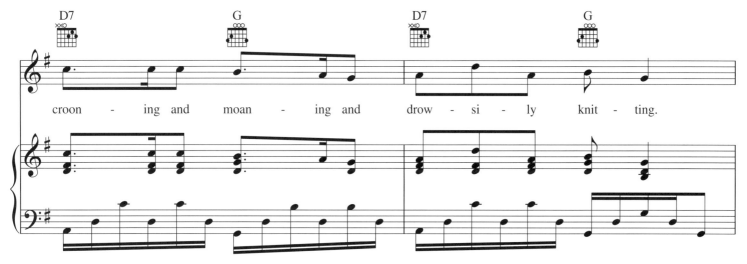

croon-ing and moan-ing and drow-si-ly knit-ting.

Chorus

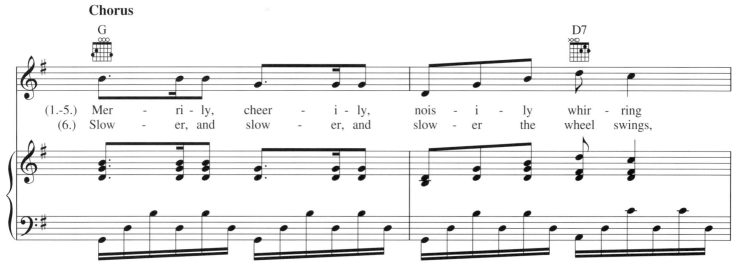

(1.-5.) Mer - ri - ly, cheer - i - ly, nois - i - ly whir - ring
(6.) Slow - er, and slow - er, and slow - er the wheel swings,

swings the wheel, spins the wheel while the foot's stir - ring.
low - er, and low - er, and low - er the reel rings;

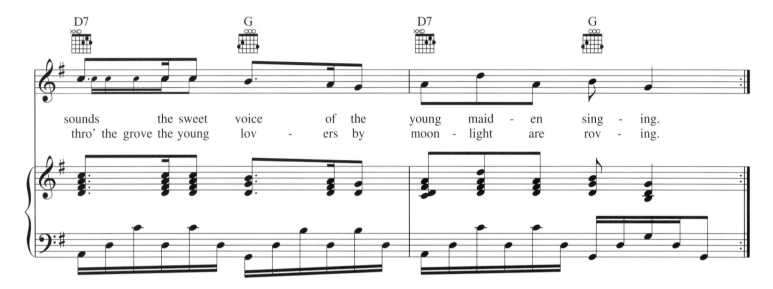

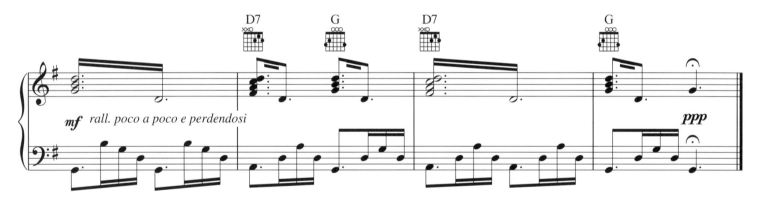

Additional Lyrics

2. "Eileen, a chara, I hear someone tapping,"
   "'Tis the ivy, dear mother, against the glass flapping,"
   "Eily, I surely hear somebody sighing,"
   "'Tis the sound, mother dear, of the autumn winds dying."
   Chorus

3. "What's that noise that I hear at the window I wonder?"
   "'Tis the little birds chirping the holly-bush under,"
   "What make you be pushing and moving your stool on?"
   "And singing all wrong that old song of Coolin"
   Chorus

4. There's a form at the casement, the form of her true love,
   And he whispers with face bent, "I'm waiting for you, love,
   Get up on the stool, through the lattice step lightly,
   And we'll rove in the grove while the moon's shining brightly."
   Chorus

5. The maid shakes her head, on her lips lays her fingers,
   Steals up from the seat, longs to go and yet lingers;
   A frightened glance turns to her drowsy grandmother,
   Puts one foot on the stool, spins the wheel with the other.
   Chorus

6. Lazily, easily, swings now the wheel round,
   Slowly and lowly is heard now the reel's sound;
   Noiseless and light to the lattice above her
   The maid steps, then leaps to the arms of her lover.
   Chorus

TEDDY O'NEIL

Words and Music by
SHAMUS O'LEARY

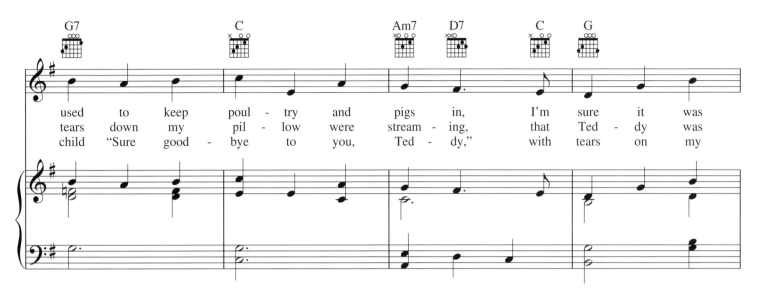

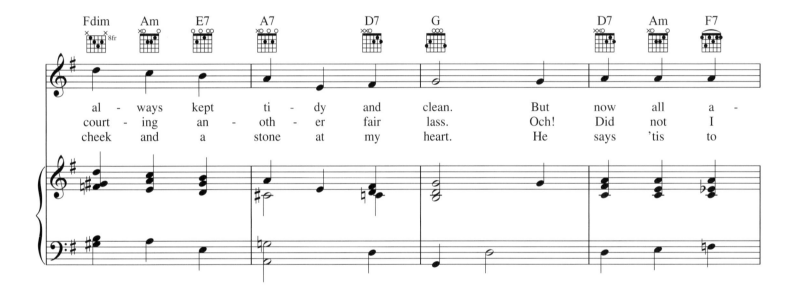

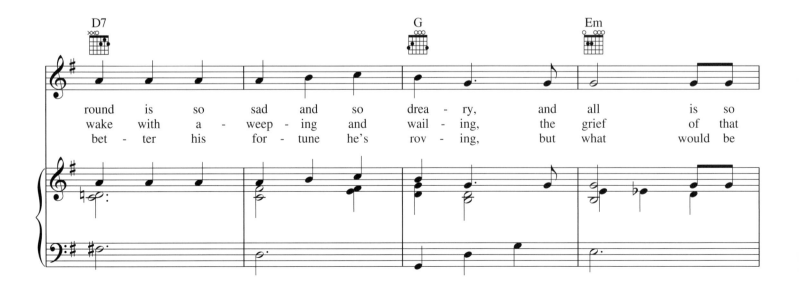

si - lent, no pi - per, no reel, not e - ven the
thought was too deep to con - ceal, my moth - er cried
gold to the joy I would feel, if I saw him

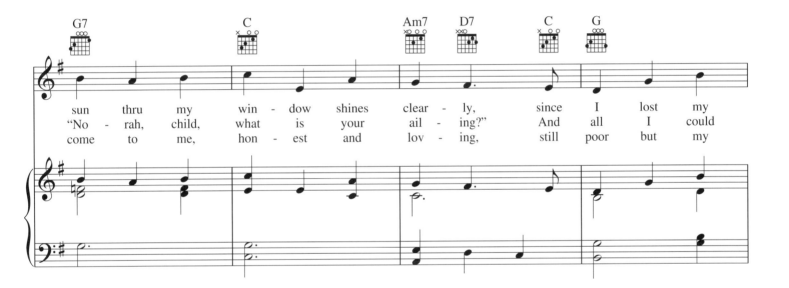

sun thru my win - dow shines clear - ly, since I lost my
"No - rah, child, what is your ail - ing?" And all I could
come to me, hon - est and lov - ing, still poor but my

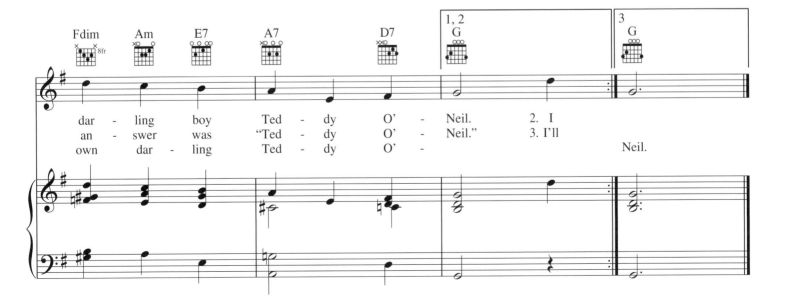

dar - ling boy Ted - dy O' - Neil. 2. I
an - swer was "Ted - dy O' - Neil." 3. I'll
own dar - ling Ted - dy O' - Neil.

THREE LOVELY LASSES
IN BANNION

Words and Music by DELIA MURPHY
and SEAMUS KAVANAGH

Lyrics:

I met a boy com-ing o-ver the hill,

o-ver the hill from Ban-nion;

Sing-ing a song com-ing o-ver the hill,

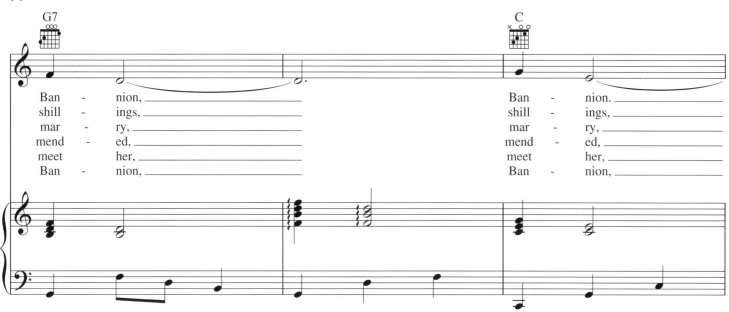

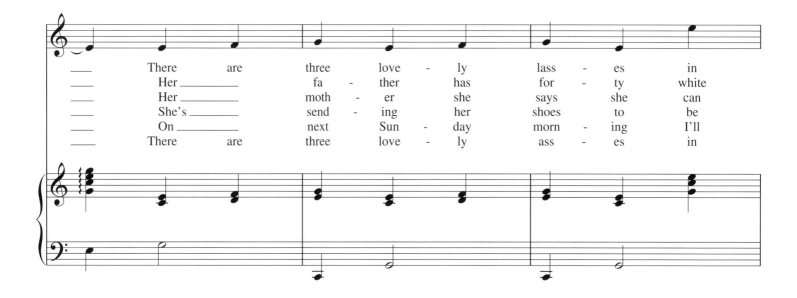

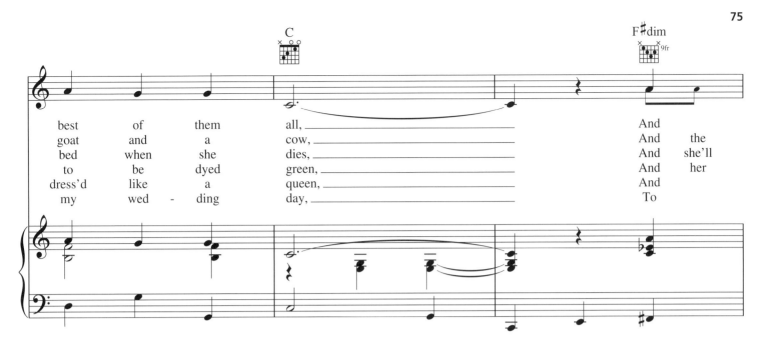

best of them all,_____ And
goat and a cow,_____ And the
bed when she dies,_____ And she'll
to be dyed green,_____ And her
dress'd like a queen,_____ And
my wed - ding day,_____ To

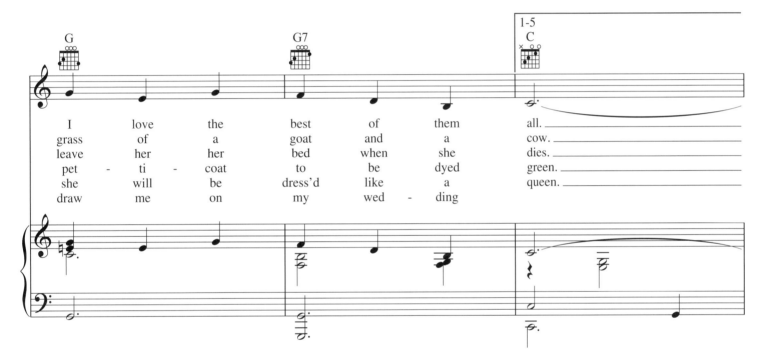

I love the best of them all._____
grass of a goat and a cow._____
leave her her bed when she dies._____
pet - ti - coat to be dyed green._____
she will be dress'd like a queen._____
draw me on my wed - ding

_____ For her day._____
_____ And her
_____ So she's
_____ And on
_____ There are

THE WHISTLING GYPSY

Words and Music by
LEO MAGUIRE

1. The gyp - sy ro - ver came
2.-4. (See additional lyrics)

o - ver the hill, Down thro' the val - ley so shad - y, He

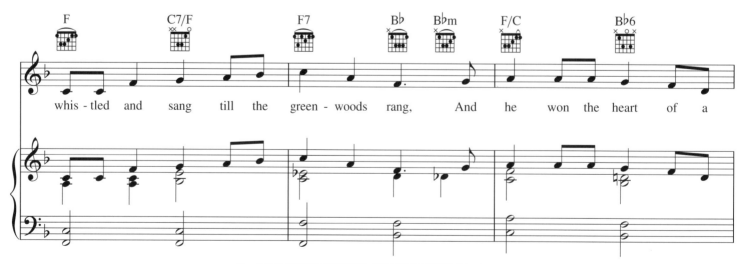

whis - tled and sang till the green - woods rang, And he won the heart of a

Chorus

Additional Lyrics

2. She left her father's castle gate
   She left her fair young lover
   She left her servants and her state
   To follow the gypsy rover.
   Chorus

3. Her father saddled up his fastest steed
   He ranged the valleys over
   He sought his daughter at great speed
   And the whistling gypsy rover.
   Chorus

4. He came at last to a mansion fine
   Down by the river Clady
   And there was music and there was wine
   For the gypsy and his lady.
   Chorus

5. "He is no gypsy, father dear,
   But lord of these lands all over
   I'm going to stay 'til my dying day
   With my whistling gypsy rover."
   Chorus

WILL YE GO, LASSIE, GO

Words and Music by
THE McPEAKE FAMILY

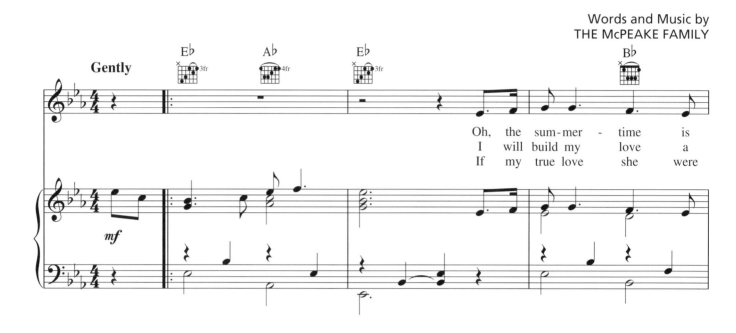

Oh, the sum-mer - time is
I will build my love a
If my true love she were

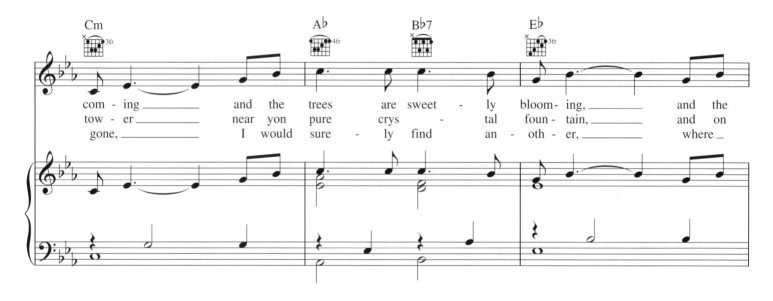

com-ing _____ and the trees are sweet - ly bloom-ing, _____ and the
tow - er _____ near yon pure crys - tal foun - tain, _____ and on
gone, _____ I would sure - ly find an - oth - er, _____ where

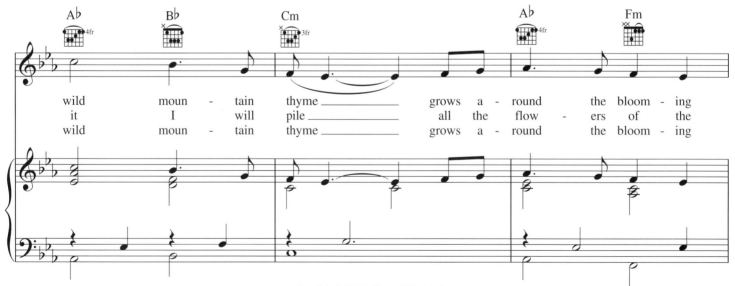

wild moun - tain thyme _____ grows a - round the bloom-ing
it I will pile _____ all the flow - ers of the
wild moun - tain thyme _____ grows a - round the bloom-ing

MORE CELTIC & IRISH SONGBOOKS

The popularity of Celtic music has soared over the last decade due to the resurgence of folk instruments, Celtic dancing, and Irish culture overall.

Learn how to play these beloved songs with these great songbooks!

THE BEST OF IRISH MUSIC

80 of the best Irish songs ever written in one comprehensive collection. Includes: Danny Boy • If I Knock the "L" out of Kelly • Macnamara's Band • Molly Malone • My Wild Irish Rose • Peg o' My Heart • Too-Ra-Loo-Ra-Loo-Ral (That's an Irish Lullaby) • Wearin' of the Green • When Irish Eyes Are Smiling • and more.
00315064 P/V/G $16.95

THE BIG BOOK OF IRISH SONGS

A great collection of 75 beloved Irish tunes, from folk songs to Tin Pan Alley favorites! Includes: Erin! Oh Erin! • Father O'Flynn • Finnegan's Wake • I'll Take You Home Again, Kathleen • The Irish Rover • The Irish Washerwoman • Jug of Punch • Kerry Dance • Who Threw the Overalls in Mrs. Murphy's Chowder • Wild Rover • and more.
00310981 P/V/G $19.95

THE CELTIC COLLECTION

The Phillip Keveren Series

Features 15 traditional Irish folk tunes masterfully arranged in Celtic style by the incomparable Phillip Keveren. Songs include: Be Thou My Vision • The Galway Piper • Kitty of Coleraine • The Lark in the Clear Air • Molly Malone (Cockles & Mussels) • and more.
00310549 Piano Solo $12.95

THE GRAND IRISH SONGBOOK

125 cherished folk songs, including: Believe Me, If All Those Endearing Young Charms • The Croppy Boy • Danny Boy • The Galway Races • Johnny, I Hardly Knew You • Jug of Punch • My Wild Irish Rose • Too-Ra-Loo-Ra-Loo-Ral (That's an Irish Lullaby) • The Wearing of the Green • When Irish Eyes Are Smiling • and more.
00311320 P/V/G $19.95

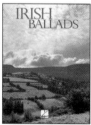

IRISH BALLADS

Nearly 60 traditional Irish ballads, including: Black Velvet Band • Brennan on the Moor • Cliffs of Doneen • Down by the Sally Gardens • I Know My Love • I Never Will Marry • Johnny, I Hardly Knew You • Leaving of Liverpool • Minstrel Boy • Red Is the Rose • When You Were Sweet Sixteen • Wild Rover • and more.
00311322 P/V/G $14.95

IRISH FAVORITES

From sentimental favorites to happy-go-lucky singalongs, this songbook celebrates the Irish cultural heritage of music. 30 songs, including: Danny Boy (Londonderry Air) • The Girl I Left Behind Me • Killarney • My Wild Irish Rose • Tourelay • Who Threw the Overalls in Mistress Murphy's Chowder • and more!
00311615..$10.95

IRISH PUB SONGS

Grab a pint and this songbook for an evening of Irish fun! 40 songs, including: All for Me Grog • The Fields of Athenry • I Never Will Marry • I'm a Rover and Seldom Sober • The Irish Rover • Jug of Punch • Leaving of Liverpool • A Nation Once Again • The Rare Ould Times • Whiskey in the Jar • Whiskey, You're the Devil • and more.
00311321 P/V/G $12.95

IRISH SONGS

25 traditional favorites, including: At the Ball of Kirriemuir • At the End of the Rainbow • Dear Old Donegal • Galway Bay • Hannigan's Hooley • The Isle of Innisfree • It's the Same Old Shillelagh • The Moonshiner • The Spinning Wheel • The Whistling Gypsy • Will Ye Go, Lassie, Go • and more.
00311323 P/V/G $12.95

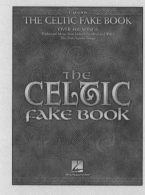

THE CELTIC FAKE BOOK

This amazing collection assembles over 400 songs from Ireland, Scotland and Wales – complete with Gaelic lyrics where applicable – and a pronunciation guide. Titles include: Across the Western Ocean • Along with My Love I'll Go • Altar Isle o' the Sea • Auld Lang Syne • Avondale • The Band Played On • Barbara Allen • Blessing of the Road • The Blue Bells of Scotland • The Bonniest Lass • A Bunch of Thyme • The Chanty That Beguiled the Witch • Columbus Was an Irishman • Danny Boy • Duffy's Blunders • Erin! Oh Erin! • Father Murphy • Finnegan's Wake • The Galway Piper • The Girl I Left Behind Me • Has Anybody Here Seen Kelly • I Know Where I'm Goin' • Irish Rover • Loch Lomond • My Bonnie Lies over the Ocean • The Shores of Amerikay • The Sons of Liberty • Who Threw the Overalls in Mistress Murphy's Chowder • and hundreds more. Also includes many Irish popular songs as a bonus.
00240153 Melody/Lyrics/Chords $19.95

FOR MORE INFORMATION, SEE YOUR LOCAL MUSIC DEALER, OR WRITE TO:

HAL•LEONARD® CORPORATION

7777 W. BLUEMOUND RD. P.O. BOX 13819 MILWAUKEE, WI 53213

Visit Hal Leonard Online at **www.halleonard.com**

Prices, contents and availability subject to change without notice.

1006